DARING
TO LIVE ON THE
EDGE

Loren Cunningham with Janice Rogers

DARING TO LIVE ON THE EDGE

THE ADVENTURE OF FAITH AND FINANCES

YWAM PUBLISHING
P.O. Box 55787 / Seattle, WA 98155

YWAM Publishing is the publishing ministry of Youth With A Mission. Youth With A Mission (YWAM) is an international missionary organization of Christians from many denominations dedicated to presenting Jesus Christ to this generation. To this end, YWAM has focused its efforts in three main areas: (1) training and equipping believers for their part in fulfilling the Great Commission (Matthew 28:19), (2) personal evangelism, and (3) mercy ministry (medical and relief work).

For a free catalog of books and materials, call (425) 771-1153 or (800) 922-2143. Visit us online at www.ywampublishing.com.

Daring to Live on the Edge
Copyright © 1991 by Loren Cunningham

Published by YWAM Publishing
P.O. Box 55787, Seattle, WA 98155

13 12 11 10 09   8 9 10 11 12

ISBN-10: 0-927545-06-3
ISBN-13: 978-0-927545-06-8

Unless otherwise noted, Scripture quotations in this book are taken from the Holy Bible, New International Version®, Copyright© 1973, 1978, 1984 by the International Bible Society. Used by permission of Zondervan Publishing House.
Verses marked NASB are taken from the New American Standard Bible, © 1960, 1962, 1963, 1968, 1971, 1972, 1973, 1975, 1977 by The Lockman Foundation. Used by permission.
Verses marked LB are taken from the Living Bible, Copyright © 1971 owned by assignment by Illinois Regional Bank N.A. (as trustee). Used by permission of Tyndale House Publishers, Inc., Wheaton, Illinois 60189. All rights reserved.

Printed in the United States of America

Contents

Acknowledgments

Every book is a team effort. We are grateful to the following people who helped make *Daring to Live on the Edge* a possibility: David Aikman, Marty Akin, David Barrett, Andy Beach, Geoff and Janet Benge, Harry Conn, Warren B. Eaton, Lucy Flach, Dawn Gauslin, Rod Gerhart, Phyllis Griswold, Chuck Hartle, Rene Hartzner, David Hazard, Paul Long, Winkie Pratney, Felicia Putnam, Jim Rogers, Jim Shaw, Scott and Sandi Tompkins, William Turner, Pam Warren, and all who shared their stories of trusting God for provision.

A Word from the Author

This book is for two readers—two very different audiences with different needs and reasons to read this book.

In one audience are the missionaries, the full-time Christian workers, or the potential workers. They need to know how to step out, to trust and obey God for finances.

In the other audience are the people in the pews, the people working in "secular" jobs. They, too, need to learn not only how to obey God but to trust Him for the miraculous.

You're not supposed to write one book for two such different audiences. But God has so designed it that His work cannot be done except in partnership.

There is much in this book for each of these key players in world missions—the one serving faithfully in the local congregation, praying and giving to God's work, and the one going out as a missionary.

Because each player is significant in God's scheme of things, I have an unusual request of you. *Will you read this book in its entirety?* While chapter 9 is directed primarily to those in the workaday world, the same principles will be important for those in full-time Christian work or missions.

Likewise, those in the workaday world will find much in chapters 11 through 14 to help them as they become partners with those in missions. You will notice throughout the book that most of our examples come from thirty-one years of trusting God to provide for mission work in over two hundred countries. However, as I have shared financial principles based on those experiences in conferences with business leaders, CEOs, and government leaders in a number of nations, I have learned that we all face the same challenges—to step out, to dare to live on the edge for God. Besides, we all need to learn more from one another so that we can have effective partnerships in fulfilling God's work on earth.

It's never easy to step out on that tightrope for God. Whether it's your first opportunity to hear and obey or your thousandth, it is always exhilarating. But once you have experienced the thrill of radical obedience, you will never be the same. I am praying that as you read this book, you will be willing to take the first step, or the thousandth, in following our courageous Commander.

LOREN CUNNINGHAM
Kona, Hawaii

ONE

Spoiled for the Ordinary

CLOUDS OF DUST FILLED the air as we bounced along the rutted roads in Ibo land, in eastern Nigeria. I glanced over at my host, Walter Kornelson, his ruddy complexion now wreathed in sweat and dirt. I would be with this older missionary and his wife for five days—five days I was really looking forward to. He was a rugged, go-for-broke evangelist, and even though I was young and just starting out in missions, I felt comfortable with the idea of holding evangelistic meetings with him. The most exciting prospect was five nights of preaching to the pagan Ibos.

"Loren, we're sure glad you came!" he said, turning his eyes from the road but never slowing down. Chickens fled, squawking in protest, from before our station wagon. "I've been preaching in one of these villages every night without a break for four months," he said, grinning. "It'll be great to hear someone else for a change!"

I nodded, about to reply, when, *bam!*, then a sickening flap, flap, flop against the hardened dirt road. The vehicle lurched, but Walt held the steering wheel tight and brought the car to a stop. I didn't need an explanation. I got out with him to inspect the damage. A tire blowout sounds the same anywhere in the world.

"Oh, Lord! What am I going to do!" Walt exclaimed, heading to the back of the car for the spare, his shoulders slumped with a new weariness.

"What's wrong? Can't we buy a tire in Enugu?" I asked.

"Well, yes, but . . . " His voice trailed off as he wrestled with wrench and lug bolts.

He didn't say much after we got back in the station wagon and limped down the road. Finally he said, "I'm sorry to let you down, Loren, and I'm sure sorry not to get to those people, but it'll be a while before we can get the money to replace this tire. With duty and all, they cost about forty-five dollars here. I don't know what we're going to do."

You have forty-five dollars, a small voice inside said. *Yes, but that's all I have!* I protested. And in five days I would leave here, and the relative security of people I knew, and fly to Khartoum, Sudan, for a two-day layover. Two days in a strange city. I'd have to have a place to stay, something to eat, bus fare . . . forty-five dollars wouldn't even be enough for that.

Then I thought, *Mom and Dad would give him the money, even if it was their last.* I had watched them trust God and give to others for twenty-five years, and God had never failed them.

"Walt," I said. "Let me pay for your tire. Let's go get it right now." He protested a little. "Are you sure, son? You have a long trip ahead of you." But I insisted, and we found a shop on a dusty side street.

It cost forty-two dollars, and I now had three dollars in my pocket, but the Reverend and Mrs. Kornelson didn't know it. We launched into five hard, wonderful days and nights. In each village, as soon as we arrived and began to set up the equipment to show our Gospel film, crowds appeared out of the bush as if by magic. Sometimes we'd have a couple thousand people by the time it was dark, pressed tightly together in front of the screen. After the film, I preached with the help of an interpreter and a hand-held bullhorn. It was great.

But my secret Saturday deadline was coming. I still had only three dollars—what would I do in Khartoum?

Each day I quietly wondered when Walt made his routine stop by their post office box. Maybe there would be a letter for me with something in it. But did anyone know I was here? Could mail find me out here in Ibo country? On the last day Walt went by the post office once more on our way out to the bush. He came ambling back to the wagon, his large frame hunched a little as he rifled through a bunch of letters.

"Look, Loren," he said, "they've found you all the way out here!" And he handed me a single letter from some friends in Los Angeles. I opened it and swallowed. One hundred fifty dollars. From someone who had never given anything to me before.

I shouldn't have been surprised at the faithfulness of God, but somehow, when you're living on the edge—trusting God and not knowing where the next dollar is coming from—it never gets routine.

I know what you're thinking. You're saying, "Sure, God came through that time, but you weren't in any real danger. You weren't in Khartoum with no money. You could have stayed on with the Kornelsons until funds arrived." Let me tell you about Evey and Reona.

Evey Muggleton and Reona Peterson believed God was leading them to Albania, one of the countries most hostile to the Gospel in the early 1970s. In 1967 Albania had declared itself the first atheistic nation in the world. They closed every church, synagogue, and mosque and had a harsh answer for those who refused to say there was no God: they sealed them alive in barrels and threw them into the Adriatic Sea.

For three years Evey and Reona prayed and planned. During one of their prayer times, Reona saw a clear mental picture of herself in Albania, as well as a tour bus and a woman's face.

Finally they were given visas to Albania, joining a tour group of mostly Marxist youth from Western Europe. They went by bus, just like in Reona's vision.

Reona and Evey smuggled Albanian Gospel portions past the border, taped to their bodies. Once inside, despite strict supervision, they were able to secretly place the booklets here and there for people to find.

One day an Albanian servant entered Reona's hotel room. To Reona's amazement, it was the same woman she had envisioned three years before! She knew she was to try to speak to the woman and give her one of the Gospel booklets. Reona broke through the language barrier in the simplest words she could use: "Marx, Lenin, no! Jesus, yes!" The woman took the Gospel eagerly and clasped it to her chest. With tears in her eyes, she said, "Me Christian, too!" and slipped the booklet into her pocket.

A few hours later, a loud knock came at Reona's door and she was taken to a dimly lit room, blue with smoke, where five men were waiting. Out came the Gospel booklet she had given to the woman. Reona's heart sank—they must have caught her new friend with it.

They began to interrogate her, accusing her of being a spy and committing crimes against the people of Albania. While Reona remained calm, insisting on her innocence, the men grew more and more agitated. Then the head interrogator exclaimed, "You are not cooperating! We will keep you here until you break!"

In another room Evey was undergoing the same harsh interrogation. It continued that way for two days and nights, for both women. They were given nothing to eat, just a little water and a few hours' sleep. Their interrogators kept them separated, screaming accusations in their faces, trying to provoke fear in them. But the women quietly maintained their innocence.

Finally one of their accusers told Reona coldly, "You are a traitor to the glorious People's Republic of Albania, and traitors are shot. We will come for you at nine tomorrow morning."

The next morning they came and roughly took them out of their rooms. However, instead of being executed, Evey and

Reona were dumped without explanation at the border, and their homeward tickets were confiscated.

It may not seem like much of a problem after they had already faced the possibility of a firing squad, but they still confronted an enormous challenge to their faith. Two young women carrying heavy suitcases would have to cross ten kilometers (about seven miles) of swampy no-man's-land on the hostile border between Albania and Yugoslavia. After that, they'd have to cover one thousand kilometers (about seven hundred miles) of Yugoslavian coastline, cross northern Italy, go over the Alps into Switzerland, and somehow make it home to Lausanne. Could they trust God to get them home with very little money, no tickets, and no knowledge of the countries or languages?

They responded in faith. After all, a God who could deliver them from a firing squad certainly could be trusted to help them find their way home.

There was a series of little miracles. A taxi improbably appeared in no-man's-land *and* the driver even agreed to take them to the border for no money. From there, they caught a series of rides using the time-honored manner of hitchhiking. But what happened just before the Yugoslav-Italian border is truly a mystery.

It was seven in the evening, and the two stood a few kilometers from the Italian border, trying to decide what to do. They had no Italian money. Was it safe to hitchhike across Italy at night?

Just then a sleek car pulled up alongside them. Evey motioned to the driver, pointing the direction they wanted to go—across the border. The man nodded and without a word loaded the young women and their suitcases into the car and sped toward the border. When they arrived to find a long line of cars awaiting inspection and passport control, their driver accelerated into a separate lane by himself and drove straight past the Yugoslavian side of the border with a small wave of his hand.

Who is this? Reona wondered. *Surely he must be a high-ranking Yugoslav official, to leave a Communist country in such a casual fashion!* But they were even more amazed when they arrived at the Italian side. Again, a long line of cars waited patiently to be cleared and admitted. This time their driver didn't even slow down or wave. He swung into an outside lane and drove straight through into Italy. Who was this man? A Communist official could have sped through the Yugoslav checkpoint, but wouldn't he have to stop and receive permission to enter Italy?

Again there were no words from the driver, only silence. The car finally stopped at an Italian village ten kilometers inside Italy, pulling up to a bus stop. He placed a large number of Italian lire into Reona's hand, looked at her, and finally spoke his first words: "Bus, Trieste; Trieste, train."

And that was all. He drove off. But with those instructions they took the bus to Trieste, and from Trieste took the train to Lausanne, Switzerland. With the little money they already had, plus that given them by the silent stranger, they had just enough to make it all the way home.

Does this story seem strange or out of reach from your experience? Is God that real and that practical, to even include exact directions home with His provision? I trust as you read this book, you will learn how you can trust Him, too, wherever you are and whatever the challenges you are facing.

There are many ways of trusting God in finances. We can learn to live by faith in His variety of provision. And we can step out and see Him at work on our behalf. Best of all, we can learn His ways. Once you've experienced the life of faith, it ruins you for the ordinary.

As people have observed the rapid growth of the number of people and ministries in Youth With A Mission, they have asked how it was possible to do so much so fast. I tell people I didn't establish YWAM, Jesus did. It is almost as if I have been an observer of what He has done. An important key to our fast growth as a mission has been the way God has led us in faith and finances. Unless you know God and His miraculous power, it's impossible to understand how it happened.

I want to share principles we have learned, to help Christians see God's ways and better learn how to trust Him. In our modern world, everybody needs money because most things you do involve money. If you are willing, God will lead you into a lifestyle where everything is done with faith in Him, including how you get and how you use your money.

This message applies to all of us. It is for

- the young family trying to tithe when their income is inadequate;
- the church pastor struggling over how to pay the staff salaries *and* fix the roof, even though offerings have fallen off;
- the high school or college graduate wondering whether to choose financial security or something better;
- the retired couple trying to make ends meet on a fixed income;
- the missionary in some lonely outpost, worrying over what to do about the money she needs;
- the person, young or old, stepping out for the first time into full-time Christian ministry, wondering if he can support himself;
- those who find themselves with some money to spare, who wonder how to best use it for God's glory.

This book is for those who long for something more, an exciting involvement in what God is doing all over the world.

Whatever your situation, my desire is to see you do anything God calls you to do, no matter how daring. But the choice is yours. You can settle for the ordinary, or you can have the thrill of a new walk with God. Are you ready to live on the edge?

TWO

Have You Ever Seen a Worried Bird?

H AVE YOU EVER SEEN a worried bird? One who had deep wrinkles in his brow? Perhaps his eyes were bleary and bloodshot, with circles underneath from many sleepless nights. Somehow you knew he had been trying to keep a stiff upper beak as he worried over how he would pay the mortgage on his nest!

Jesus was the One who used birds as an example of the way we should face the subject of finances. He said in Matthew 6:26:

Look at the birds of the air; they do not sow or reap or store away in barns, and yet your heavenly Father feeds them. Are you not much more valuable than they?

No, you haven't seen a worried bird! We can learn from the birds the secret of living like this. Jesus told us we were not to be anxious for what we would eat or drink or for the clothes we needed. In fact, He said our lives should be different from those of unbelievers who run after these things. We are to be as carefree as the birds of the air.

Is this true of most of the Christians you know? Is this true of you? What if you were to lose your job tomorrow, or if your business were to go bankrupt, or your investments were to go sour? What if God were to call you to sell everything you have and serve Him in missions? Could you trust Him for your needs?

This is what many Christians call living by faith—they mean missionaries or ministers of small churches who have no salary and perhaps no regular donors or income at all. However, I want to extend this term. Jesus wants us all to live by faith, as we'll see in coming chapters of this book. Everyone—those with salaries and those without—have the privilege of seeing God provide for their needs.

But first, what is faith? And how do you get it? Is faith squeezing your eyes shut and believing with everything in you that Santa Claus is real? No matter how hard you believe, Santa Claus will never be real. Such an idea is pure fantasy. On the other hand, God is real whether or not you believe in Him. His existence and power are not related to how much faith you have.

Does faith require you to turn off your mind and fling yourself off some cliff of impossible circumstance? Hardly! Søren Kierkegaard popularized the term "a blind leap of faith." But Bible faith is neither *blind* nor a *leap*. It is *walking* in the *light*.

The Bible says faith is the assurance of things hoped for, the evidence of things unseen (Heb. 11:1). In other words, faith is believing that something will happen before it happens. Faith is believing that you will have what you need even if you have nothing. Faith is a strong assurance in God's character, knowing that even if you can't see the solution to your problem, God can.

Bible faith is not wishful thinking; it's not based on wanting your selfish desires so badly that you somehow get "faith" and get them. Neither is it some concentration of your mental or spiritual "powers" to get something you want.

Bible faith comes from

- knowing what God wants you to do,
- obeying whatever He shows you to do, then
- trusting Him to do what you cannot do, in His way and in His time.

There is a hymn that is often sung, "Trust and obey, for there's no other way. . . . " I would suggest we switch the order of the words—"Obey and trust"—and let the Lord go into action.

According to Romans 10:17, "Faith comes from hearing the message, and the message is heard through the word of Christ." Faith is based on hearing what God has to say to you in His written word, the *logos*, and in His quickened, specific word to you personally, the *rhema*. Bible faith isn't declaring some ridiculous thing, then waiting for it to happen. Even if He asks you to do something that appears to be impossible, it will never be foolishness. Bible faith starts with hearing God. The true leading of the Holy Spirit, the *rhema*, never contradicts either the *logos* or the character of the One who wrote the *logos*.

Knowing what God wants you to do is the first part of Bible faith. The second is taking steps of obedience that He shows you to take. Bible faith requires action on your part. It isn't passive.

A remarkable example of this happened some years ago while we were living at our School of Evangelism in Switzerland. I was in an intercessory prayer group with several young workers when the Lord impressed upon me that our mission was going to get a farm. It was a total surprise—we weren't praying for a farm—but the word came very clearly to my mind. By that time YWAM had several properties being used for missions training and outreach. I told our small group about this impression, and together we asked God to let us know whether it was from Him. My mind quickly went to work on the idea. I could see how a farm could be a great place to train young missionaries as well as provide food for them and others.

Soon the word of the Lord was confirmed to one or two others in the prayer group. We finished our time by thanking God, and we trusted Him to bring it about.

The next day was Saturday, and as I headed out into a misty spring morning to jog, I passed by a farm near our school. An auction was going on, and all the farm implements were being sold off. Instantly I knew I was to do something—an act of faith to follow through on what the Lord had promised the day before. I went back quickly and got Joe Portale and Heinz Suter, two of our French-speaking staff. We returned to the auction in time to buy a wagon, a roll of barbed wire, and a milk can.

We hauled the wagon home by pulling it like a trailer behind our car. Then we parked it on the lawn in front of our school and put the other things away until God gave us our farm. I guess it could look foolish to some people, but we were simple enough to believe God had promised it and would do it.

That weekend, one of our European YWAMers went home to her parents for a visit. She told her dad, a Swiss pastor, "God just told us we are going to have a farm!"

Some parents might have been amused or even critical of such a statement, but this young woman's father just happened to be on the board of a ministry that was situated on a beautiful farm (valued at over a million dollars at the time). The leaders of that ministry had been sensing for some time that their work was completed. They had been searching for three years for a Christian organization to give the farm to.

So we were given a million-dollar farm, free of charge. Our biggest expense in getting it had been the one thousand Swiss francs I paid for the wagon, the roll of barbed wire, and the milk can! For twenty years now, this farm in Burtigny, Switzerland, has served as a place for discipling young people and providing food for many missions workers. The wagon remained as a lawn decoration in front of our school until it was moved to the farm, where it finally fell apart from the effects of weather. Even then, Heinz Suter (who now leads the work at the farm) saved a piece of the wagon and used it as background for a decoupaged scripture plaque he gave to me. That plaque is a constant reminder that God will provide if I take steps of obedience whenever He speaks.

Think of the great miracles of the Bible. They often required steps of obedience first. The walls of Jericho fell down, but only after seven days of marching. The Chaldean general was healed of leprosy, but only after he had traveled for days and then dipped himself seven times in the Jordan River, as instructed by the Lord's prophet. Jesus sent the blind man to wash his eyes in the pool of Siloam before he was healed. Peter was told to go fishing for money—and he found it in the mouth of a fish. Specific steps of obedience released the miracles.

The third part of faith is trusting God to do His part.

Whenever we speak of trust, we have to know the one we're being asked to trust. Imagine a salesman coming to you, asking you to sign a contract, and saying, "You don't have to read all that fine print or know everything about my company and the services we're selling. *Just trust me!*" Would you trust him? Could you?

That is why trust and faith in God's Word have to be strongly grounded in knowing His character and His track record. Study the attributes of God in the Bible. Go through His promises in the fine print of the contract. Read stories of His faithfulness, both in the Bible and in modern times. Write down all the times in the past when you know God came through for you. Then, when you are deeply convinced of His absolute trustworthiness, you can have faith.

Sometimes living by faith means waiting, giving Him the opportunity to act. A farmer described it to me like this: God tells you to go out on a limb. Once you get out there, you hear a sound—*rrrh! rrrh! rrrh!* You turn around, and there's the

devil with a chainsaw, cutting off your limb. Bible faith is staying on the end of that limb and watching Satan continue to
saw until the whole tree falls over with him in it and you stay
aloft on your limb! That's faith. It's not faith in the tree or faith
in the limb. It's faith in the Word of God and faith in the One
who stands behind His word.

Many Christians never prove God's trustworthiness in this
category of their lives; they remain financially self-sufficient,
never stepping out on a limb, never doing anything out of the
ordinary. Instead, it seems, they ask their bank accounts, "Oh,
Bank Account, will you allow me to do this for God?"

Those who listen to God will find themselves doing things
they can't complete without His help. They will take steps of
obedience, then allow God to do His part. In other words,
Bible faith requires that you do the possible and let God do
the impossible. Faith only operates when we have no other
resource but God.

Let me tell you about one young man who went out on a
limb. David Snider was in the Virgin Islands helping us provide oversight for teams of young volunteers on various islands
during our Summer of Service. When David traveled to St.
John to buy supplies for one team, he found the provisions
cost more than anticipated. He was due back in St. Thomas by
Sunday for meetings but had used all the team's finances and
had none of his own. He prayed with the team on St. John,
and they all felt he was to go ahead and return to St. Thomas
in time for the Sunday meetings. The only question was, how
would he pay his fare?

The day came to leave, and David still had no money. He
remembered from his trip over that fares were collected halfway through the voyage. He went ahead to the dock, pausing
before going up the gangplank. Had he really heard God cor-
rectly? Again, a calm voice inside said, *Yes. Go!*

He found a seat on deck among the seventy other passengers and soon was talking to the people next to him, a Carib-
bean doctor and his wife. They inquired politely about his

purpose in traveling among their islands, and David explained simply: he was here with a group of other youths, talking to people about God.

The time passed quickly—all too quickly for David, who managed to keep a nonchalant air as he visited with his new friends. What would they think when he was caught as a stowaway after sharing with them about the Lord? Soon he spied the man from the shipping company coming along collecting fares. David continued in pleasant conversation, glancing down the deck to note the man's progress toward him.

All too soon he was there, facing David. As David reached into his empty pocket, the doctor said, "No, here, let us pay for your fare!"

You may never find yourself in David's situation. Then again, you may find yourself in circumstances that demand just as radical an intervention from God. How can you make sure that God will hold you up when the devil saws off your limb? The key is obedience to God and having a personal knowledge of the One you are trusting.

God may call you to take a job with a salary. If you obey Him, it can lead to a life of faith. If you keep listening to Him, asking Him how to use your salary, and obeying Him in all areas, you will be living by faith.

He may lead you to make investments. If they are done in the will of God, you are living by faith whether you end up with a profit or a loss. I know one businessman who has been led to make investments inside the People's Republic of China for a number of years now. He has lost money on *every one* of these ventures, but the Lord has enabled him to make money elsewhere so that his enterprises inside China can pave the way for Christians to go into the country to evangelize. He has also become friends with some of the government leaders, sharing his faith with them. I would say that my friend is a faith missionary in every sense of the word.

God may call you to go to a country as a missionary in the more traditional sense. He may lead you to share your goals with others in order for them to give toward your work. Or He may tell you to go with no money in your pocket, no contacts in that country, no place to stay or work when you get there. Either way, the key to living by faith is not in a method. The key is to hear, obey, and trust God. As we obey Him, He gets intricately involved in our lives. And since money affects almost all areas of life, God will enter into our finances in many exciting ways, if we let Him. You have heard the saying "That is something you can take to the bank!" Faith in God and His word to you is that certain—you can literally take it to the bank.

THREE

Why
Live by Faith?

WHY DOES GOD WANT us to live by faith? First, living by faith proves to us and to the world that God is real.

When I was a student at the University of Southern California, I had a professor of philosophy who seemed to be trying to tear down his students' faith in God. He was a brilliant yet embittered son of a minister. He had lost his faith and tried throughout the semester to challenge anyone who had faith. There were questions he posed that I could not answer at the time. But there was one thing I could never deny, and that was my experience. I had seen too many things happen that could only have been done by God.

I believe this is the primary reason God led us in Youth With A Mission to ask each worker to trust God for his or her own financial needs, that is, food, drink, and clothing (the needs Jesus specifically mentioned in Matthew 6:31–33), as well as travel costs. Scores of thousands of workers from over one hundred nations have gone all over the world, taking up that challenge and believing that where God guides, He provides. And where He leads, He feeds!

At first I worried. God's guidance was so clear, yet the three or four other mission groups I was closest to paid salaries, at least for their secretaries and home-office people. But the Lord told us there were to be no salaried positions in Youth With A Mission. Everyone—from myself to the youngest volunteer, from the evangelistic team member to the mechanic fixing the group's bus —was to trust God for his or her upkeep and travel.

I have never thought this was the only way to run a missionary organization. It was just the way God led us. Much later I learned that almost all mission boards with more than a handful of missionaries in the field operate on this same basis, each individual trusting God and being personally responsible for raising his own living and ministry expenses.

Before long we realized why God was leading us this way. We gained clear confidence that God was real. Whether we were confronted by angry Marxist students at a Latin American university or by the smug indifference of European intellectuals, we knew God was real. He had to be or we couldn't have gotten travel funds to get there or had anything to eat after we arrived.

The amount is not important when you're trusting God. If you don't have the money you need at the time you need it, a ten-dollar shortfall might as well be a million-dollar one. Once while Darlene and I were still newlyweds, we were traveling through Chicago to our next meeting in Wisconsin. Our money was running out fast, partly because of the numerous toll roads. Yet, if we were to make it on our tight schedule, we had to take the toll roads. Every few miles, it seemed, we were having to slow down and put one more quarter from our dwindling supply into the hopper.

"Well, look, Dar!" I said, as I fished what was left out of my pocket, pulling up to the last toll booth. "Thirty-five cents. That's twenty-five cents for the toll, and one dime to call Pastor Wilkerson when we arrive in Kenosha." She laughed as I dropped the quarter in and sped onto the turnpike. "Praise the Lord! We just made it!" she said. I agreed, but my joy was short-lived.

We hadn't gone far before there was another sign telling us to slow down and be ready to pay another toll. *Lord, what will we do?* I looked over at Dar, but she was already shaking things out of her purse, looking to see if a coin had somehow eluded her. We needed twenty-five cents, and we needed it now. Just then a thought came to me. *Pull over and open the back door.* I did. And there, between the door and the frame of the car, was a quarter standing on end. What a big quarter! I've never seen a bigger quarter in my life.

Was it a coincidence? I don't think so.

At other times the need has been far greater. Early in our ministry, Darlene and I were in Edmonton, Alberta, Canada. We received a phone call from our secretary back in Pasadena.

"Loren, I don't know what we're going to do," Lorraine Theetge said, the strain in her voice obvious even in the long-distance connection. "We haven't had any income in quite a while, and our accounts payable due right now come to $5,200!"

I told her we would try to do something. But when I hung up the phone, I felt totally overwhelmed. It had been touch and go financially for months, and all of a sudden it was too much to face.

I threw myself across the bed in the home where we were staying. "God," I cried out, "this need is yours. I can't handle it!" A few moments later, the phone rang shrilly. It was Lorraine again.

"Guess what happened, Loren?" Lorraine's voice rang over the wires. "We got a check for two thousand pounds from a bank in England." She went on to say that it was from an anonymous donor in a third country, and that the British bank was merely forwarding it to our office. "And you know what else, Loren? I called our bank and asked for today's exchange rate of British pounds to dollars, and this comes to exactly $5,200!"

A coincidence? Not on your life!

Proving God Is Real

My friend Brother Andrew, known to many as "God's Smuggler," puts it this way: Suppose you were walking through a jungle, and unknown to you, a lion is stalking you. Just as it springs through the air, a coconut falls from a tree, knocking the lion out cold. You turn, surprised and relieved. It could be a coincidence, just good luck. But what if it happens again the next day? Another lion leaps, only to be hit by another falling coconut. And the next day, still another lion and one more lucky coconut. How many times does this have to happen before you know it's not a coincidence?

In our mission we have more than twenty thousand short-term volunteers each year, plus more than seven thousand full-time staff, working to share the Gospel out of permanent ministry bases in over one hundred countries. Mobile teams have gone with God's love to every populated country on earth. Over and over again, these people are seeing similar "coincidences" of good fortune. Some of us have experienced them for decades now. Let me share one team leader's story with you. His name is Neville Wilson, a Fijian born and raised in New Zealand and now the leader of YWAM in Tonga and the South Pacific.

"We were in a pioneer situation in Nadi, Fiji. Our seven team members were Fijians. We couldn't get any foreigners in as staff because of the visa situation. When we heard that visitors were coming through, we would often walk the five kilometers (3.1 miles) to the airport. We didn't have the finances to take a taxi. But each time, God provided for us to bring our visitors home in a taxi.

"For instance, once, while meeting someone's plane, we met a local friend at the terminal who gave us a donation without knowing our need. God would provide for us to have extra food for visitors, too. And we'd even have enough money to take them back to the airport by taxi. Then we'd walk home after they left, laughing over how God had done it again.

"Our YWAM center was a house like our neighbors', out in the cane fields, furnished mainly with mats on the floor. One evening we were sitting around, and a local woman came in with five loaves of bread. That would feed the seven of us for several days. But fifteen minutes later someone else knocked at our door, wanting to give us some bread. Then a neighbor came with more bread. Within one hour we had been given two dozen loaves of bread.

"'Why do we have so much bread?' my wife asked. 'Maybe someone is coming.' It wasn't an hour later that we heard that a group of fifteen people was arriving that night from New Zealand."

At other times, God gave Neville and Sue more than bread, and more than real necessities. It was Christmas Day in 1979, and they were in Maui, Hawaii, on an evangelistic team with a number of others. Neville sat on the front porch of the house where they were staying, feeling lonely. His father had died a few weeks before. Neville remembered how his dad had always provided a ham for their Christmas dinner.

Neville thought, *Oh, I'd love some ham right now*. A few minutes later, a black pickup roared up, carrying a load of rough-looking local Hawaiians. To Neville's surprise, they pulled right onto the property in front of his house, and one big guy stood up and threw a ham at him, saying, "Merry Christmas!"

The Word of God says in 2 Chronicles 16:9, "The eyes of the Lord range throughout the earth to strengthen those whose hearts are fully committed to him."

My philosophy professor at USC taught that it was impossible to prove a philosophical negative. But you can prove a philosophical positive. God's Word says He is faithful and that the righteous will never go hungry, nor will their children ever have to beg for bread (Ps. 37:25). That is a philosophical positive that can be proven—lived out in dollars and cents. Moreover, faith isn't real unless it can be proven practically in the real, everyday world.

A remarkable experiment to prove the reality of faith was undertaken by a young Scotsman named George Patterson in the days after World War II.

It all started with three young men and an argument in a restaurant. George contended that the Bible was the Word of God. Every word was true. His second friend was an agnostic, refusing to take anything so unscientific as authoritative. His third friend was a nominal Christian, unsure that the Bible was the Word of God, or even which parts of it might be the Word of God.

The lively discussion continued awhile, drawing the curiosity of fellow diners. Then George had a bold idea. He declared to his two friends that he would prove the Bible scientifically. He took his wallet out of his pocket.

"I say there is a God, and this God has revealed Himself and His purposes for men, in and through His Word." He emptied the contents of his wallet on the tablecloth and counted. There were two pounds and seven shillings.

George looked his friends in the eyes and declared, "I will give away all the money I have in the bank. Not only that, I will divest myself of my savings bonds." He told them he was due to leave soon for his medical studies, preparing himself for missionary service.

"I will take with me only these two pounds and seven shillings plus my last paycheck. While in London during the next months, I will have no resources nor financial support. I will only have the Lord.

"I make you a promise," he said solemnly. "I will not tell a single person, other than you two, what I intend to do so that this will be between the three of us and God. I will not tell my parents nor let it be known to any church or missionary body. I won't dress differently or alter my style of living so as to suggest by implication that I am short of money . . . anything I require will have to be supplied by God. If I have to ask a single person for help, I promise you I will return home, and never again mention the sufficiency of God or my belief in Him."

George Patterson thus entered into what he called "The Gamble" with "naked belief in the Omnipotent." During his gamble, as far as anyone knew, he was merely a student from a well-heeled family going to school on his own expense without any needs.

Yet immediately God began to send people to him with small amounts of money. They would say, "God told me to give you this" or "Take this as from the Lord." It always varied, but it was always there, although at times within mere minutes of when it was needed.

There was one exception: the money did not come for a necessary trip home. Since he didn't have enough for the entire fare from London, he went as far as he could, then walked for two days to reach Scotland. Patterson later said he thought this was a test of his faith. He believed God wanted to see how desperate he could get and still keep on trusting Him.

It was more than the gamble of a student, eager to prove himself right to his friends. George Patterson's experience of trusting God while a student would prove very necessary when he went to Tibet. At that time Tibet had no link with the postal union. Conventional means of missions support would be useless. He would also face Tibetan priests with impressive occultic powers, and then imprisonment and persecution at the hand of the Communist Chinese as they took over the country. His entire story was told in his book, *God's Fool*. But before he ever set foot in Tibet or China, he had proven the Bible to be real. He had gambled and won.

Seeing Your Faith Increase

If the first reason to live by faith is to prove the reality of God, the second reason is to see our faith increased. All of us are given a measure of faith, according to Romans 12. Faith is a gift, but it must grow through use. Faith increases as we exercise it. It's like physical exercise. The difference between the Arnold Schwarzeneggers and the rest of us is their commitment to increase strength and muscle mass by exercise. "No pain, no gain," they remind us as they throw a hefty medicine ball our way.

There was a time in my life when I was extremely weak and debilitated. For days I could not lift my head off the pillow. One day I was able to lift my head a little bit. I continued doing that, for it was all I was able to do. After a time I grew strong enough to turn in my bed. After more months I was able to move about but only by crawling. I could not stand or walk. Then one day, after I was a year old, I was finally able to stand up and walk.

Even then there was a problem working against me. It was called gravity. I would take a few steps and fall down, again and again. Yet as I worked every day, pushing against that force of gravity, I grew steadily stronger and fell less. Finally I could even run and jump.

I realize my experience is far from unique. But have you ever thought about the process God designed for us to go through as infants? Wouldn't it have been easier without gravity? Toddlers could leap and float about instead of struggling to stand. But that struggle is necessary to help develop our growing muscles.

Similarly, if we never have needs in our lives, if we can do everything without God's help, how can we learn to trust Him? The disciples in Luke 17:5 cried, "Increase our faith." They had seen Jesus do so many miracles. Surely He could instantly impart faith to them. But they had to go through the same process we do. Like life breathed into us, faith is a gift from God. But for our faith to increase, it must be used and tested.

Sheila Walsh is known to millions through her music ministry and her position as co-host of the Christian TV program "The 700 Club." But before she was a household name to so many, she was a girl who stepped out and had her young faith tested. Sheila heard about an outreach YWAM was planning during the Summer Olympics in Montreal in 1976. As a student at the London Bible College, she longed to go and share her faith with Olympic visitors from all over the world.

The only problem was, she didn't have the money. She says, "Back then, I hardly had enough money to buy a new pair of Levi's, let alone a plane ticket to Canada!" However, she prayed and felt a strong assurance that she was to go to Montreal. Sheila also believed she was not to share her need with anyone but simply to pray.

Bit by bit, during the intervening weeks, the money came. People began to give her small amounts of money. It added up to almost all that she needed. Sheila had enough for her round-trip airfare from London to New York, with some left to take a bus on to Montreal. But for her return to New York, she still needed seventy dollars.

Sheila wasn't too worried. Hadn't God already provided hundreds of dollars for her to go? She went to Montreal and enjoyed two weeks of outreach along with our other sixteen hundred volunteers from many nations. Each day she went out to the streets and parks of Montreal to share her faith. And each day she waited to see how God would get her home.

Near the end of the event, I assembled all sixteen hundred workers for an open-air meeting on the lawn in front of the old mansion we had purchased for a training center. Although I didn't know Sheila yet, I knew there were many young people there who had trusted God and come on a one-way ticket. I asked anyone who had financial needs to stand and walk to the front of the crowd. Hundreds streamed forward. Then I told everyone to bow their heads and ask God to tell them which person to go to and how much to give.

"And don't rule out giving, just because you have needs yourself," I reminded those standing in front.

Sheila remembers thinking, *Great! This is where I get my sixty-three dollars!* She already had seven dollars. But to her surprise, Sheila received a strong impression to give away her seven dollars. *That couldn't be God*, she thought. *It would certainly be irresponsible to give away the only money I have!*

However, the Holy Spirit continued to nudge her until she could no longer deny the guidance. She walked casually around the group, who were all bowing in earnest prayer or already hugging someone and handing him money. It was a wild, wonderful scene.

Who do you want me to give my seven dollars to, God? Sheila prayed. Then she saw a young blonde girl and felt she was to give her the money. As Sheila pressed the seven dollars into her hand, the blonde gave her a big squeeze and beamed, "That's exactly what I needed!"

Encouraged, Sheila found her way back to her place. But by now the meeting was ending and people were drifting off. *What about my seventy dollars, Lord? I don't understand! I really trusted You. I was obedient, and now I'm going to have to live in Canada for the rest of my life!*

She found a quiet spot by the bank of a small river behind the YWAM center. There she sat and poured out her complaint to God. After a while she heard Him speak inside her: "Sheila, do you trust Me, or do you only trust what you can understand?" She ducked her head and let the tears flow, asking God to forgive her for her unbelief.

The next morning everyone was packing up to leave. Vans and buses were pulling out for the airport, the bus or train station, or YWAM centers in other parts of North and South America. Sheila walked out into the sunshine with her backpack, sleeping bag, and empty pockets. She thanked God for a new day and for what she was learning about the security of trusting Him.

As she waited outside with the others headed for the bus depot, she heard someone calling her name.

"Sheila Walsh? Sheila?" She turned, and there was one of the young women who had worked on the administrative staff. "There was a mistake in the amount you paid for your time here," she explained. "You overpaid." Sheila opened the envelope that was thrust into her hand. She pulled out seven ten-dollar bills. Then the bus came to take her to the depot.

Such dramatic provisions and miracles don't happen every day, but the ones that do serve to remind us of God's faithfulness for years to come. Such special provisions do not prove our spirituality, but they do prove to us that God is great enough for any circumstance or test.

The Lord led the Israelites in the wilderness for forty years, providing food from the sky, water from a rock, and clothing that didn't wear out. He told them why He did this: "Remember how the LORD your God led you all the way in the desert these forty years ... to teach you that man does not live on bread alone but on every word that comes from the mouth of the LORD" (Deut. 8:2–3). God is still wanting a people who will live this way, not trusting in their own means to provide a living for themselves, nor in some earthly system, but in Him.

Many nations today are on the verge of bankruptcy. The world economy is fragile, held together by one government having faith in another, by one individual having faith in another, and by people having faith in a currency because of the government backing that currency.

After one of my father's yearly checkups, the doctor pronounced him "sound as a dollar!" Dad replied with a twinkle, "Now I'm worried, Doc!"

We can't have our faith in any human systems. They will fall. You may invest in insurance plans or annuities or stocks and bonds. These things are not wrong. But don't put your faith in them. Put your trust higher than man. I find that people with a selfish bent can't help but destroy, sometimes even in an attempt to help others. I don't trust man. But I do trust men and women of God, and I trust the Lord. I also trust God to rule and keep even the wicked under control.

We need to see God as our true source. The natural tendency of the human heart is always toward independence, away from dependence upon God and others. Is this why Jesus told us to pray, "Give us this day our *daily* bread"? Notice, He did not say we were to ask for next week's bread, just in case. Daily dependence upon God allows us to know we're in His will and obeying Him. We can look daily to God rather than man.

Those who are trusting God to provide for their needs while in ministry must especially keep this in mind. It is easy to get our eyes on those whom God has used in the past to meet our needs. When in a financial crunch, we can even resent those who aren't giving, if we're not careful. We must fight the tendency to rely on the seen world instead of the unseen world. What is unseen is really more secure and reliable. God said heaven and earth would pass away, but His word would never pass away. He loves us and is concerned with every area of our lives and every need. And He will prove Himself to us and to the world by taking care of us.

Listening to God and Learning His Ways

Another reason for living by faith is to learn how to listen to God and obey Him. The Lord said our heavenly Father knows what we need before we ask. So why does He want us to ask? The Lord wants to keep the lines of communication with us open. If we are trusting Him for finances, He has to lead every move we make. He has our full attention and so can teach us about His character, His ways, and His power. Remember, the people of Israel knew the *acts* of God, but Moses knew His *ways* (Ps. 103:7). He wants us to really know Him in depth so we can trust Him more. And He will set up situations so that we can learn His ways while receiving provision for our needs.

In 1972 we planned to have our largest evangelistic endeavor up to that time, in Munich, Germany, during the Summer Olympic Games. However, the biggest obstacle we had to overcome was housing. We expected one thousand workers from all over the world. But where would we house them? All hotels, youth hostels, boarding rooms, and even private residences with extra rooms had been booked for months.

It was several months until we needed housing for workers. A more pressing need was where to put our printing press. Money had been donated for evangelistic literature, but it was more economical to buy a Heidelberg press and print literature ourselves, with volunteer staff. The large press would be delivered in days, and we had no place to put it. We sent out two young men, Gary Stephens and Doug Sparks, to look for a place.

Gary called me from Germany. "Loren, we found a place for the printing press ... "

"What is it, Gary? A shed?"

"Well, yes, but it's attached to a sixteenth-century castle in a town called Hurlach. The castle is for sale!"

Somehow, as soon as he said that, I knew the castle was for us, even though we had no extra money to buy anything.

I went with two friends, Don Stephens and Brother Andrew, to meet with the owners. On the way there, God impressed me with the amount we were to offer and when we needed to take possession. When we met with them, I simply told them our terms: we would give them the first payment of 100,000 Deutsche marks (about $31,000) in ten days, but we needed to move into the castle the next day. (We had no choice. The press had to be delivered the next day ... to somewhere!)

The owners were taken aback, but they went aside to confer. They returned in minutes, agreeing to our offer and handing us the keys to the castle. "You certainly have an unusual way of negotiating for property," one of their attorneys said. "You go about it like you were buying ice cream cones."

It did come easy. We took possession of the castle that night. Within a week, 100,000 Deutsche marks came in from various sources in Europe. People felt led to send it to us. And we moved in—immediately, hours before the Heidelberg press arrived. It was so easy.

I thought, *This is great! God speaks to us and gives us the terms; the people agree to it; then God leads people to give the money. We move into a property and use it for ministry.* I expected it to be that easy every time.

However, God was wanting to teach us His way, which is to trust in Him, not methods. That means our experience will be different almost every time. Just how different we were soon to learn.

Lynn and Marti Green left our center in Switzerland to pioneer a work in Great Britain. Lynn called one day, excited about a property he felt God wanted to give them.

"It's incredible, Loren," he told me over the phone. "A great big old English mansion—big enough to hold one hundred staff and students. It's called Holmsted Manor. I would have never picked something so big, but Marti and I and our board members have prayed, and we feel this is from God."

Great, I thought. *Another castle.* God was so good, and this business of trusting Him and buying big properties was so easy.

I flew to Heathrow Airport, where Lynn, Marti, and seven of the YWAM United Kingdom board members met me. I had been praying, too. I agreed with them that, yes, this was from God, not just human excitement or desire.

We drove to Crawley and then to Holmsted Manor, thirty-seven miles from the center of London. I wasn't prepared for the old elegance of the three-story mansion, which was surrounded by other buildings and thirteen acres of land. The asking price was around 60,000 pounds (US$144,000 at the time). This included 5,000 pounds for the furnishings in the main house. The owner had divided up the original estate. Three acres with a swimming pool and football field on one side of the driveway and three acres on the other side of the drive were being sold separately. What was left was a guitar-shaped piece of land, with the guitar's neck being a long, tree-lined driveway leading to the stately manor house and main buildings.

We left our van out on the highway and walked down the drive and into the huge old place, admiring the hand-carved oak paneling and the stained glass windows in the entry hall. Something inside me said, *This is what I want to give you for a missionary training center for Britain.*

After inspecting the main buildings, several of us decided to march around the perimeter of the property, praying for God to give it to us. We slogged through the muddy, plowed land in great excitement, praising God that He would release the money needed. (At the time, YWAM UK had only two hundred pounds in the bank—just enough to pay for having the place surveyed.)

As we concluded our "faith walk," rather than going back down the tree-lined drive to the highway, we decided to also troop around the parcels adjacent to the "neck of the guitar"— land that wasn't included in the proposal—the three acres with the football field and swimming pool and the three acres on the other side.

After our prayer march that day, Lynn and Marti began telling other Christians in England of our plans to buy Holmsted Manor as a missions training center. Within four months, six thousand pounds came in—enough for the deposit. It seemed like it was going to be another easy faith conquest, like the castle in Germany.

It would come at just the right time, too. Lynn and Marti and their staff of twenty-two were housed with various friends, and in a few days scores of summer volunteers would arrive to share their faith on the streets of Crawley. Lynn and Marti had no idea where they would put all the workers.

However, we were in a special training course all our own, set up by the heavenly Father. He was more interested in our learning His ways than in our easily taking properties for His work. Unexpectedly, to our confusion and dismay, the Holmsted Manor property quickly sold to someone else!

We went back to the Lord and asked, "Why is this happening? We thought you said it was for us, for a missions training center." There was no answer, only the quiet assurance that He *had* spoken. Holmsted Manor was to be ours.

He confirmed this by inspiring Christian friends to give toward the purchase of Holmsted Manor, even though they knew the property had already sold. The balance of the sixty thousand pounds came in, and we carefully salted it away in a separate bank account.

In the meantime, Lynn was able to rent a large house to accommodate the summer workers. In the fall we continued our pursuit of Holmsted Manor. We were desperate. By this time Lynn and Marti and forty coworkers were housed in a small house in London, sharing one bathroom on a highly regulated schedule!

The ministry continued to grow. They had teams going into central London and other areas, and they continued to offer special training opportunities in their small rented house. It was often comical. Once a Bible teacher from the United States gave several days of lectures in their largest room—a bedroom thirteen feet by fifteen feet, lined all around with bunk beds. The students sat on the bunk beds and the serious, dignified Bible scholar stood near the window, preaching his heart out.

Months passed, but God never let us give up. Holmsted Manor passed from the first owner to another—for three times the price we had originally offered!

In the meantime, our growing YWAM staff moved from place to place. Finally we leased Ifield Hall, another distinguished but slightly decaying mansion, about six miles from Holmsted Manor. Again the arrangements were made just before another crop of summer volunteers arrived to do evangelism. The only problem was, there was no furniture in Ifield Hall.

Less than a week before the volunteers arrived, Lynn made another foray to Holmsted Manor, just out of curiosity. As he pulled up, workers were carrying out the furniture. When he inquired, the foreman explained that the new owners were opening an exclusive boys' preparatory school and wanted new furniture.

"What are they going to do with the old furniture?" Lynn asked, remembering that this was the very furniture for which we had offered five thousand pounds in our original proposal.

"Oh, I guess they're going to put it up for auction."

"Can I buy it?" Lynn asked. The foreman must have carried some authority because he asked, "How much?" Lynn took a deep breath and said, "One hundred pounds." The foreman took off his cap and looked around at the workmen, still carefully unloading the furniture from the house to the circular driveway. He shoved his cap back on his head, looked at Lynn, and countered, "Two hundred pounds." They ended up agreeing on one hundred fifty pounds, and the YWAMers gleefully collected the furniture for which we had originally agreed to pay five thousand pounds.

"We felt just like Joshua and Caleb, bringing back those giant grapes from Canaan!" Lynn reported. To us, that furniture was a pledge on our future inheritance of Holmsted Manor.

But still, as months lengthened into years, it was hard to explain the delay to donors who had believed with us for Holmsted Manor and given sacrificially toward its purchase.

Once during those years, Lynn met me at London's Heathrow Airport. We sat in his parked car and prayed for God to allow us to make some sort of apology to the public and return the sixty thousand pounds in the bank to the donors. We must have been mistaken, we thought. The Lord hadn't said Holmsted Manor. He had given us Ifield Hall instead. In fact, by this time Ifield Hall was filled to overflowing with one hundred staff and families.

But the Lord wouldn't let us off the hook. Even though He assured us that it was right to have Ifield Hall, He gave us quiet confidence that His word had not changed from four years before. We would have Holmsted Manor too. We could easily understand how Joseph felt in Egypt, where he was tested by the Word of the Lord (Ps. 105:19 NASB). It would have been easier to simply apologize and say we blew it.

Finally, in the summer of 1975—four years after we had taken our muddy prayer walk around Holmsted and the adjoining acres—word came from the owners. They would accept our original offer of sixty thousand pounds!

Also, the bits of land on either side of the guitar-shaped property had been added during those intervening years. Now, for sixty thousand pounds, we could get the property we originally tried to buy *plus* the three acres with the football field and swimming pool and the other three acres of farm land—the parts we had included in our prayer march four years earlier.

After we moved into Holmsted Manor, we had another march—this time a march of praise with 175 YWAMers tramping over the land. We had gained so much more than a valuable property to use in the training of young missionaries. We had learned much about God's ways.

- He showed us that when He speaks, even though circumstances say otherwise and things go wrong, He is the one who brings things to pass. However, it wouldn't always be as easy as buying ice cream cones.
- We learned, as the Lord added Ifield Hall to us, that sometimes His word is not either/or but this/and that too.

And we learned many other things, including the fact that our heavenly Father was far more interested in us than in properties. He would rather teach us His ways, and see our character grow and our faith increased, than to immediately provide for our needs.

If God cares more about us than He does about money, what place does money hold for us? Does God have anything to do with money, or is it just the spiritual realm He is concerned with? We will see in the next chapter how these two realms—the spiritual and the material—are connected.

FOUR

God and Money

REACH IN YOUR POCKET and take out a dollar, if you have one. Unfold it and look at it. Look at the front, at the pictures and engraving. Turn it over and look at the curious markings on the back. It is paper—engraved with a blending of black and green ink—a high quality bond with tiny threads of red and blue in it. It's just paper and ink. The United States government grinds out 1.6 billion one-dollar silver certificates each year. Another 5.4 billion notes in fives, tens, twenties, fifties, and one hundreds are printed every year. Great blankets of green roll over the presses and are cut, neatly bound, and shipped to reserve banks all over the country.

It's another commodity. The same presses could just as easily print bumper stickers. But the presses print money— paper stuff to allow the value of one person's work or product to be converted into a form that can be carried in a pocket and traded for other goods and services he or she needs, even halfway around the world. Money.

However, something about these engraved pieces of paper can destroy a marriage or cause men and women to sacrifice leisure time with family and friends, and even health, to get more of them. This innocent paper you're holding has driven young men in the inner city to entice their friends to take killer drugs. It has corrupted the justice of men who started out to give their lives upholding the law. The lust for money has led adults to do unspeakable things to children, to make millions in the kiddie-porn trade. The desire for wealth has even caused wars. Somehow money has the terrible ability to gain control of a person's soul.

The power of money can bring life or death. Let me tell you two stories.

Nearly twenty years ago, a man in Southern California gave two thousand dollars for a YWAM property to be purchased in the South Pacific nation of Fiji, not far from the airport in Nadi. For years the property waited there. Finally, in 1983, a team led by Neville Wilson came to pioneer a permanent work in Fiji. (We told some of Neville's story in the previous chapter.) They began to build on the property—a simple building, much like those lived in by their neighbors, in the sugar cane fields. That building has been used for numerous ministries, including the launching of a twenty-four-hour prayer chain to pray for the evangelization of every nation on earth. So far they have prayed around the clock since January 1, 1989—over twenty-four thousand hours of prayer for such places as Mongolia, Saudi Arabia, and Russia.

There has never been much money at the base, but they have high ambitions to affect nations. Eight Fijian missionaries have gone out to nations like India. They want to make a difference in Fiji, too, so they have started a preschool to help the poorest of the children on the island—the children of the cane field workers, many of whom are from India.

In Indian elementary schools in Fiji, children who do well academically are given the honor of sitting in the front of the classroom. Those who do poorly have to sit in the back. The locals say a cane field worker's child has never been able to sit in the front of the classroom. For generations, they have done the worst and have sat in the back. Now, thanks to YWAM's preschool, cane field workers' children sit in the front! And some of their parents have been converted from Hinduism to faith in Jesus Christ.

All of this—children with a new future, parents with a new faith, young missionaries sent out after a three-year-plus prayer meeting for the nations—because a man from California invested two thousand dollars in God's work far away in the Fijian Islands. It almost seems as if the money has taken on life—like a seed planted that God has caused to grow.

Money is not always given so freely, nor does it always bring life. It can bring death as well. Let me tell you the second story.

Last year a pillar of orange fire and billows of black smoke poured into the night sky of Austin, Texas, as firemen arrived at a blazing two-story apartment building. While the fire engines wailed to a halt, people dressed in pajamas, underwear, and even bed sheets ran from the building. A young firefighter looked up in horror as an obviously pregnant girl stood screaming inside a second story window. Then, responding to urgent cries in Spanish from a young man already on the ground, she jumped, landing with a thud and a whimper.

The firemen hurried to connect their hoses and advance into the searing heat, but experience told them it was too late to save the building or anyone trapped in it. It was an explosive fire, probably started from kerosene or some other flammable substance.

From the ground floor, a woman and a man came stumbling out as walking torches. Paramedics ran to cover them with blankets, smothering the flames, trying to comfort them and gently help them into ambulances.

"No, no, I can't go!" screamed the woman, her face charred and streaked with tears, "My baby is in there! I've got to get her out!"

But by then their apartment looked like the inside of a furnace. Sadly, a young medic shook his head and firmly urged her toward the ambulance.

It was almost morning before they found the remains of a fifteen-month-old girl in the still-smoking ruin. But before they found the baby's body, the authorities had learned the horrible truth about the cause of the fire.

A man, angry because someone would not repay him eight dollars, had shot a flare gun into the building through a window, igniting some flammable substance. A building was burned to the ground, forty-eight people were homeless, seven people were hospitalized, and a baby was dead—all because of an argument over eight dollars.

Why does money hold such power over men?

What does God think of money? Does He see it as a necessary evil? Didn't Jesus put God and money in opposite corners when He told us, "You cannot serve both God and Money" (Matt. 6:24)?

Money is not evil, though the love of money is. Paul said the love of money is the root of *all* evil (1 Tim. 6:10 KJV). There's nothing wrong with money itself. But because of the sin in men's hearts, the love of money can lead to pain and bondage—even for Christians. Money is like a chameleon—it takes on the color of its owner's heart. There is such a thing as contaminated money or "blood money." Even the chief priests understood this, refusing to put Judas's money back into the treasury.

However, money itself is not evil. It's just paper stained with ink. Money and God are not on opposite sides, either. In fact, God uses money as a practical tool for many things. He uses money or the lack of it to test us, to see what is in our hearts. How we use our money is a gauge of where our priorities are.

When a person wins a state lottery, one of the first questions reporters ask him or her is, "What are you going to do with the money?" What we don't realize is, God asks us the same question over every dollar put into our hands. What we do with it shows our character. If we are faithful with our money, Jesus says we will be entrusted with spiritual riches as well (Luke 16:11).

God also uses money to teach us to trust Him. Remember how Elijah was led by the Lord to a brook where he hid out for some time during a severe famine? No doubt he quickly settled into a routine—he knew about when to expect the ravens with his breakfast and dinner each day. He sat by the cool stream in the shade of its bank. Then slowly but definitely his brook dried up.

God didn't allow him to become comfortable trusting in that brook, even though it had been God's provision for him. He was ready to lead Elijah somewhere else, so He caused Elijah's brook to run dry.

When our financial brook runs dry, we are ready to listen to the Lord, who wants our willful dependence on Him. His only aim is to teach us and to bring us closer to Him. We so easily move into a greater degree of independence than God sees is best.

We need to realize that the lack of money is just as definitely from God as the provision of money. Recently, while I was on a trip to some developing nations, our personal "brook" seemed to dry up for a while. Darlene was home in Hawaii, and it hadn't occurred to her how sparse our financial flow had become. Then one day there was no money in the bank. There was nothing in any purse. And yet she had planned to go out to eat with some friends. She ended up scrambling through every drawer in the house, looking for stray coins—not many, just enough to at least pay her own way at the restaurant.

"The Lord had my attention," Dar told me later. "So I asked Him why we had no money." As Dar quieted her heart and listened, the Lord said, *It's been some time since you were trusting me for small daily needs, like toothpaste. Thousands of young people in YWAM are going through this every day. I just wanted to remind you that your needs and theirs are being met by Me.*

I have heard of other people's brooks drying up—some much more drastically than in this temporary situation of ours. One man poured out his heart, telling how he and his wife had shared the needs of their ministry in churches for one year and yet had not received a single commitment of support. Not one dollar. I thought I could discern some of the reasons for this, but it was for him to press in and get understanding from God.

However, I did know one thing. Such a dramatic lack was a miracle, too. It was as much a miracle as a sudden, abundant release of finance. For such a winsome, honorable couple to share their need for one year and not have one person or church give anything to them—that was miraculous.

When the brook dries up, we need to ask God how to move on, like Elijah did.

Because money is important in our lives, God's Word devotes much space to it. In fact, there are 3,225 references to financial matters in the Bible. We don't have to wonder what God thinks about money and its use when we search the Scriptures. In a later chapter, we will see what the Bible has to say about some of these important areas. With these foundations, we can go on to do whatever God leads us to do in complete freedom.

Many get-rich plans promise financial freedom. God promises financial freedom, too, but His freedom is quite different from the empty promises of brokers and salesmen. He promises that we will know the truth and the truth will make us free. And that includes learning the truth about money. We can be truly free.

But first we need to learn some things about our adversary and money. God isn't the only one concerned about money. Our enemy, Satan, also has great involvement in finances—acting both on a big, international scale, and personally, against us as individuals.

FIVE

The King of Wall Street

But those who want to get rich fall into temptation and a snare and many foolish and harmful desires which plunge men into ruin and destruction. For the love of money is a root of all sorts of evil. (1 Tim. 6:9–10 NASB)

THE YEAR WAS 1851. California had been a state for just over a year. But something glittering and bright yellow had been discovered in the pristine rivers of the north. Something that grabbed men and changed them. Gold!

A man named Colonel Reddick McKee was sent to head up one of three exploratory parties appointed by the Bureau of Indian Affairs. His party traced their way northward up the Klamath River to Scott Valley, the home of the Shasta Indians. They were warmly welcomed by these Native Americans, who had also been kind to the few miners who had already come. Unlike more warlike tribes, the Shasta people were gentle and friendly, simple and trusting.

Colonel McKee called a meeting with the Shasta to work out a treaty, some kind of agreement that would allow them to retain their rights as more white men came—a flow certain to increase, McKee and the government knew, because of the discovery of gold. Three thousand Shasta warriors responded to his call for a meeting and camped near Fort Jones.

Finally, the negotiations were complete and thirteen Shasta chiefs signed the treaty, along with Colonel McKee and other witnesses.

"And now, we would like you to be our guests at a giant feast!" announced Colonel McKee through an interpreter to the throng of Indians. "We call it a barbecue! We want to host you at a great meal and seal our friendship."

Some of the Indians didn't come to the barbecue. They didn't trust Colonel McKee and the white men. But most did go that day. Thousands of Indians filed by the long tables, receiving platefuls of freshly sliced meat and small loaves of bread. They sat in the crisp fall sunshine in small groups and began to eat. Only a few noticed that their hosts, the white men, ate nothing. Neither did a few Indian women, those who were married to miners.

The next day, a doctor riding a stagecoach through Scott Valley saw some odd shapes on the side of the road. The driver stopped and the doctor quickly climbed out, realizing with sick dread that the crumpled heaps were dead bodies. But nothing in his life had prepared him for what he saw when he looked down the road. Hundreds of dead Indians lay along the trail, their bodies still twisted from some agony.

At first the doctor was afraid they might have died from some sort of plague. But they had died on their way home from the barbecue, the victims of beef and bread laced with strychnine. Before the end of the day the doctor and others found more than three thousand dead. One of the few Indians who survived, Tyee Jim, helped bury the bodies. It was reported in the *Alta News*, from Alta, California, dated November 5, 1851. No official investigation of the massacre was ever conducted. The gentle Shasta Indians were no more. It was much simpler, after all, than worrying about treaties and land rights in the days of the California Gold Rush.[1]

As horrible as the Shasta Indian massacre was, it only represents a tiny part of the evil spawned from Satan since the dawn of time. Evil that is often bound up in the lust for wealth. If we are not careful, we can shrug off a scripture we have heard many times—the verse that says, *the love of money is a root of all sorts of evil.*

Ezekiel 28:12–19 gives us a fascinating glimpse into the past, before Lucifer rebelled and became Satan. Note how the lust for wealth was somehow involved in his rebellion. Also, mark the opulence described:

> Son of man, take up a lamentation over the king of Tyre, and say to him, "Thus says the Lord GOD, 'You had the seal of perfection, full of wisdom and perfect in beauty. You were in Eden, the garden of God; every precious stone was your covering: the ruby, the topaz and the diamond; the beryl, the onyx and the jasper, the lapis lazuli, the turquoise and the emerald; and the gold, the workmanship of your settings and sockets, was in you. On the day that you were created they were prepared. You were the anointed cherub who covers, and I placed you there. You were on the holy mountain of God; you walked in the midst of the stones of fire. You were blameless in your ways from the day you were created until unrighteousness was found in you. *By the abundance of your trade* you were internally filled with violence, and you sinned; therefore I have cast you as profane from the mountain of God. And I have destroyed you, O covering cherub, from the midst of the stones of fire. Your heart was lifted up because of your beauty; You corrupted your wisdom by reason of your splendor. I cast you to the ground; I put you before kings, that they may see you. By the multitude of your iniquities, in the *unrighteousness of your trade* you profaned your sanctuaries. Therefore I have brought fire from the midst of you; it has consumed you, and I have turned you to ashes on the earth in the eyes of all who see you. All who

know you among the peoples are appalled at you; you have become terrified and you will cease to be forever.'" (NASB, emphasis mine)

The Bible tells what we need to know, but it doesn't always tell everything. We aren't told how Lucifer became engaged in trade, nor with whom he traded. But he had some sort of supervisory role over wealth. This passage calls him "the king of Tyre."

Evidently the prophet Ezekiel was given a prophecy with dual reference. Part referred to the actual king of Tyre, a human leader of the top trading nation of that day. But part of the passage referred to Lucifer. No human king could be said to be "in Eden," nor be an "anointed cherub" on the "holy mountain of God." These references in Ezekiel 28 clearly belong to the one who came to be known as Satan.

How would we describe this role of Satan today? We wouldn't call him the King of Tyre. We would probably call him the King of Wall Street. You see, Satan is trying to control the trade of the entire earth. He controls people through their lust for money. Through unrighteous trade he endeavors to control not only business but science, technology, and health care; politics and government; the media; arts, entertainment, and sports; education; even churches and families.

Satan uses these tactics to enslave men financially: greed, the lust for power, pride, and fear—especially fear of financial insecurity.

When we think of greed, we may think of a rich, miserly man. Some Scrooge-like miser, sitting on piles of money, running his fingers through his coins and bills. However, greed is more prevalent among the poor and the not-so-rich. The ones most consumed with lust for ownership are the ones who have the least. Greed leads parents in India to break their infants' legs so they can use them as beggars, eliciting more pity as cripples. In America, inner city kids are killing other youths just to get their expensive athletic shoes.

Those who control wealth, on the other hand, are more tempted by the lust for power over others. They use their wealth to manipulate the poor through the greed of the poor. Recently a shoe store owner in Connecticut declared bankruptcy. He said it was because of a sign that he had placed in his window, telling drug dealers he did not want their business in his store. Several months before, he had been contacted by representatives of the manufacturer of one of the hottest lines of athletic shoes. They told him they were opening several new stores in his city. When he objected that there would not be enough demand in that area, the representatives told him, "Get some new customers. Go for the drug dealers. They will buy our most expensive shoes."

However, the man refused to do this. He went bankrupt. The newsman interviewing the merchant asked him how he could tell which customers were drug dealers. He said, "When a young man in his late teens or early twenties drives up in an expensive sports car, steps out wearing thousands of dollars worth of gold chains, and strolls through your shop pointing out your most expensive shoes, pays in hundred dollar bills and doesn't bother to wait for his change . . . you kind of get the idea where he got his money."

But who are the men behind this greed? And what are they after? You can only own so many pairs of shoes, so many TVs and VCRs, so many cars and homes. Then it becomes the lust of the game itself—the power over others that money brings.

Pride is another way Satan rules people and their finances. Have you ever heard sales pitches that promised you "the pride of ownership"? One television commercial presents a luxury car, with a silky-voiced narrator purring, "What will feed your spirit?" Such a blatant appeal to pride is reminiscent of Satan, the King of Tyre, whose heart became lifted up and corrupted as he gloried in his splendor.

The King of Tyre also controls people through their fear of financial insecurity. There is the fear of not having enough money, the fear of loss of control, and the fear of losing spending power. If fear keeps us from obeying God in anything He tells us to do, then we are vulnerable to the manipulation of the King of Tyre.

For example, the king of unrighteous trade can incite a dictator to invade another country and tie up 25 percent of the world's supply of oil. This strikes fear in the hearts of the business world from Tokyo to New York to Frankfurt. The price of oil jumps, even though there is still ample supply. Investors start to lose confidence. Interest rates on new loans go up. People stop buying. The flow of money is slowed or even stopped. Recession or a depression begins—all because of fear poisoning the atmosphere. Fear by itself can throw national economies into confusion and panic, resulting in millions losing their jobs.

Satan, therefore, rules people through the area of finances, using greed, the lust for power, pride, and fear.

What are we to do about this? Are we to steer clear of the financial districts of the world, keeping our minds on more heavenly things? Do we abandon world trade to the enemy? I don't believe this is God's will in any way, no more than it is His will for us to abandon the schools, offices of government, or places of influence in the arts, media, entertainment, and sports. These are the very areas we are to go into. Through prayer and by taking whatever righteous action the Holy Spirit leads us to take, we serve Jesus' kingdom and cause. Jesus came to redeem the earth, individual by individual, and institution by institution. And we need not fear the King of Tyre, as long as he has no leverage or device through which he can control us. Jesus said to Satan, "You have nothing in me" (John 14:30 NASB).

The finances of the world operate on buying and selling, supply and demand. This demand is often based not on real need but on the greed, lust, pride, and the fears of men. However, the kingdom of God is radically different and more powerful. The kingdom operates on giving and receiving. People who listen to the Holy Spirit, obey the Lord, and freely give are diminishing the power of the King of Tyre.

This kind of giving shakes Satan's control in the earth. We break the gridlock of greed with Spirit-led generosity. We counter the spirit of manipulation and control by having a servant heart. We meet pride with humility and quiet dignity. And we come against fear with God's perfect love, just as light drives back darkness.

When John the Baptist came preaching before the coming of the Messiah, he told his audience to repent, saying that the axe was being laid at the root of the trees and every tree that was not good would be cut down. When they responded and asked what they must do to repent, John linked generosity to what he had just said about laying the axe at the root of the trees. "The man with two tunics should share with him who has none," he said, "and the one who has food should do the same." To the tax collectors he said, "Don't collect any more than you are required to," and to the soldiers, "Don't extort money and . . . be content with your pay" (Luke 3:11–14). Almost all of the specific acts of repentance centered around money.

Generosity, then, was linked to repentance and to the cutting down of the roots of evil trees.

We have seen this in a practical way. When we first entered into negotiations on the property for our Kona, Hawaii, campus of the University of the Nations, we were led to counter greed with generosity. The story is told in detail in my book *Making Jesus Lord.*[2]

The Evangelical Sisterhood of Mary had a similar experience. Mother Basilea Schlink is the founder of this ministry, which began in Germany in the dark days following World War II. The Sisters of Mary maintain religious communities that emphasize a life of worship, trusting the Lord for their daily needs. With a handful of mostly young, Protestant nuns, they bought their first property in Darmstadt. The women learned to do the building themselves. They trusted God for the income to build gradually: first a chapel, then other buildings for a retreat center for visitors from all denominations to come and seek the Lord.

However, there was a small, odd-shaped piece of land right next to their property. The sisters became convinced in prayer that this property should be purchased for a Jesus Workshop. They were able to get all the necessary pieces of property but this one.

It belonged to an elderly woman who refused to sell or trade for any other property. The old woman maintained that under no circumstances should people give up what they inherited from their parents.

One time Sister Eulalia went to the elderly woman's house, hoping to persuade her. The woman wasn't at home, but a grandnephew was. He led the nun into his great-aunt's room. One glance told her that this woman would never part with anything as long as she lived. The room was crowded with furniture, more than any one person could use or even maintain. Enough furniture to furnish an entire house was in that one room. Most of it was dilapidated. Then the grandnephew showed the visitor the ladder that his great-aunt used to climb into bed. Her bed was a pile of mattresses inherited from her ancestors, each on top of the other. Evidently this woman had never given up one item that she had inherited.

When Sister Eulalia brought back her report, the Sisters of Mary decided that any person so bound to the things of this world could only be freed by earnest, heartfelt, continued prayer. Much more was at stake than a field of land to build a house of worship. A soul was in bondage. They decided to fast, remembering that Jesus said, "But this kind does not go out except by prayer and fasting" (Matt. 17:21). In addition to giving up food, there was also to be fasting of a different sort— giving up something much more closely related to the elderly woman's bondage.

The Sisters of Mary were already living very simply. They didn't have much money and had hardly any personal possessions. But each sister sought the Lord, asking Him to show her if there was any such spirit of hoarding in her—any attachment to an item that was greater than her attachment to Jesus.

For one it was a little wooden cross; for another it was a pretty picture postcard. The monetary value wasn't important, but the attitude of clinging was. After their "surrender week" an emissary from the sisterhood visited the elderly neighbor once more.

She couldn't believe her ears when the woman said, "I'm not too much sad about the land, but it's the plum trees; I do hate to lose the plum trees!" She was saying she was willing to sell that odd piece of property to them, but she was going to miss the plum trees on it. God had done a miracle.

They drew up a contract for the land purchase, stipulating that everything on the trees went to the old woman. And each year thereafter until she died, they sent her all the plums.

Satan is controlling the wealth that rightfully belongs to God. Our most powerful warfare against him will come as we surrender to the Lord and obey Him in detail. It is obedience, not sacrifice, that the Lord wants (1 Sam. 15:22). Often our obedience will mean sacrificial giving. But it is not sacrifice that defeats the enemy; it is obedience to God. It is not wise just to empty your pockets. I read of one poor widow who was shocked by the revelation of lavish spending by a ministry to which she had given. "And to think," she said, "I ate nothing but popcorn for one week, sending that minister my food money!"

Even if you only give to ministries that are reputable and make certain they are not wasting your gift, you cannot give to everyone. God is not telling everyone to give away everything he has or to try to meet every need. What He wants is obedience to His prompting. And if He occasionally tells you to give away everything, then He will miraculously provide for your needs.

Obedience in giving is an act of spiritual warfare. For instance, if a person in Chicago responds in generosity, giving away his money—say, to help with a missions project halfway around the world—the forces of Satan are driven back in Chicago. The amount is not important, but the attitude is. Any amount—even a widow's mite—given selflessly and in obedience batters the powers of darkness right up to Lucifer himself. Giving selflessly means that the gift will not help the giver in any way. It's not given so that he or she can have a more comfortable pew or a safer neighborhood. It is given *away*, and only God can return the blessing to that giver. This kind of giving shakes Satan, loosening his control in the country receiving the gift but even more in the country of the giver.

This is why Christians in Asia and Africa and Latin America need to be taught to give to missions and to the poor and needy in other countries. Unless we teach developing nations the power of giving, the poor will be kept poor.

This is what makes Christmas so special, even to those who understand nothing of God or His Son whose birthday we celebrate. Christmas, despite all the commercialism and other trappings, is still a season of giving and generosity. And something happens because of all that generosity—the economy is blessed for at least the next five months each year.

Giving sacrificially—to the point where you are trusting God to meet your needs—also drives back Satan in the area of fear. Your faith in God as you listen to Him, do what He tells you to do, then wait in simple trust for Him to provide for you, directly counters the King of Tyre's manipulation through fear. Face the fear of financial insecurity head on and put your trust directly in God. You will learn through experience how faithful He is.

I had a curious example of learning to give up spending power in one particular area for three years. God met my needs directly. In this case, it was my need for clothing. Jesus promised that our heavenly Father, who clothes the lilies of the fields, will certainly give us nice, suitable clothing.

During the earliest years of our mission, a woman came up to me after my message in her church and offered to buy me a suit. I imagined she would write out a check or meet Darlene and me at a shopping mall, where I could pick out a suit. But it turned out she was a seamstress in the menswear section of a Sears department store. After she got my measurements, she watched for a good buy, bought the suit with her discount, altered it to fit me, and mailed it to me.

It was a wonderful provision because as a speaker I needed a good suit now and then. Over the next three years she sent me three or four good suits. But while this met a definite need and they were always good, serviceable suits, I found it was also a "tailor-made" test from God to my pride. I never got to pick out the suits. It was a small lesson but very personal between me and God. He was showing me to give up that small right, that area of choice, to Him. He adequately supplied my need and taught me His faithfulness to meet my needs. It was just for a time—only three years. But I learned that God would take care of this most basic need as I surrendered my rights.

What the King of Tyre fears most is people who surrender their rights and place their trust in God. Satan has nothing to hold over us if we have repented from greed, if we are continually responding in generosity and giving freely with no strings attached. What can he do if we have turned away from pride, humbled ourselves, and flung ourselves into the care of God without fear? What can Satan do? What power can he hold over us, our finances, our career decisions, or our business enterprises? There will be nothing left of his power. As it predicts in Ezekiel 28, he will be turned to ashes on the earth in the eyes of all. You can almost hear the incredulous laughter of men in Isaiah 14:16, where it predicts a future day when everyone sees Satan for what he really is: "Is this the man who shook the earth and made kingdoms tremble?" We don't have to wait for that day to see Satan for who he really is. We can see it now by seeing God for who He is and becoming impressed with Him. In obedience to His leading we can strip the King of Tyre of his influence over individuals, communities, institutions, and nations.

SIX

How to Keep from Crashing

CLEVELAND CENTER, THIS IS 346 Alpha Charley. I'm at ten thousand five hundred feet. I'm in the clouds . . . not instrument rated. Would like radar vectors. Out."

—"Six Alpha Charley, Cleveland. Roger. Understand you are not instrument rated. Set transponder code 4582 for radar identification. What is your heading now, sir?"

"Six Alpha Charley is heading 250 degrees. Say again code. It's rough. I'm getting disoriented. . . . I can't see the ground!"

—"Six Alpha Charley, Cleveland. Set code 4582. Concentrate on your attitude indicator, sir. Keep your wings level and reduce power to start a slow descent. We have you on radar contact."

"I'm losing control . . . losing it . . . turning . . . I'm going to spin! . . . I'm spinning! . . . which way! Help! Help!"

—"Six Alpha Charley, release your controls, sir! Look at your attitude indicator. Opposite rudder, opposite rudder . . ."

"Help! Help! I can't stop . . . "

—"Six Alpha Charley, Six Alpha Charley, do you read?"
(Silence)

—"Radar contact is lost."

The above was based on the recorded conversation between a control tower and a small plane that crashed, killing the pilot. The investigation of this crash revealed that nothing was wrong with the flight instruments in N346 Alpha Charley.[1] The pilot, untrained to fly without outside visual references, became disoriented and lost control of his aircraft. His instrument panel contained all the information he needed to complete his flight safely. What was lacking? The training and discipline to ignore what his instincts were telling him and to fly only by reference to an outside source of information, his instruments. Which way was up? The reality he perceived as true was false. His senses had betrayed him, and it cost him his life.

In order to learn to live by faith in the area of finances, we must rely on an outside source of information, not just on our own perception of the circumstances. It's like flying an airplane on instruments. The view ahead is sometimes murky and bleak, but we can stay right side up and on course with the correct information. That source of outside information is the Word of God.

The written Word of God gives us many principles to guide our finances. I'd like to focus on the most basic ones. These truths are foundational, whether you have a job in the nine-to-five world or you're launching into pioneer missions.

Principle #1: Don't Worry About Money

One of the primary commands of the Bible is not to worry. It is just as definite as the command not to steal or not to commit adultery. The words "fear not," or similar phrases, appear approximately one hundred times in Scripture.

Jesus specifically told us not to worry about money in His Sermon on the Mount. What we were told and what we were not told of what Jesus said and did was divinely directed. Therefore, it is significant that so much space was given to this one command in the Sermon on the Mount. Think of all the evils of the world that Jesus could have warned us about. He could have called our attention to the common faults and failings of men or to the amount of suffering in the world. But He zeroed in on our preoccupation and worry over money.

Perhaps you are presently facing a financial crisis. Listen to Jesus' words as if you have never heard them before:

> So my counsel is: Don't worry about things—food, drink, and clothes. For you already have life and a body—and they are far more important than what to eat and wear. Look at the birds! They don't worry about what to eat— they don't need to sow or reap or store up food—for your heavenly Father feeds them. And you are far more valuable to him than they are. Will all your worries add a single moment to your life? And why worry about your clothes? Look at the field lilies! They don't worry about theirs. Yet King Solomon in all his glory was not clothed as beautifully as they. And if God cares so wonderfully for flowers that are here today and gone tomorrow, won't he more surely care for you, O men of little faith? So don't worry at all about having enough food and clothing. Why be like the heathen? For they take pride in all these things and are deeply concerned about them. But your heavenly Father already knows perfectly well that you need them, and he will give them to you if you give him first place in your life and live as he wants you to. So don't be anxious about tomorrow. God will take care of your tomorrow too. Live one day at a time. (Matt. 6:25–34 LB)

It couldn't be any more plain than that. One person put it succinctly: "Worry is faith in the devil." Read Psalm 37. Its key message is to not worry over finances. Three times this psalm says, "Do not fret"! It also says in verse 8 that worry leads to evil.

Whether your financial worries are the result of something out of your control, like the economy or layoffs, or the result of something you did, like the overuse of credit cards, the Bible command still stands. Don't worry over money. God will show you what steps to take to overcome your financial morass. You may also need to seek financial counseling and take steps of repentance and restitution if your money problems stem from financial abuse or lack of wisdom. But you are not to worry. Worrying will only result in wrong attitudes and wrong actions.

Choosing not to worry will require as much power of will as it would for a pilot to rely on his instrument panel rather than his own senses while flying through fog. One woman who chose not to worry over money was Lillian Trasher.

Lillian Trasher went to Egypt in the early 1900s, simply on the word of the Lord—without the formal approval or financial backing of any mission board. There this young single woman's heart was seized by the needs of thousands of orphans and abandoned children. There was no way she could do anything to help them, for she didn't have a sure source of income for herself, much less for dependent children. But she was convinced that God was telling her to do something.

She began to take in children in 1911, and soon she was responsible for fifteen hundred to two thousand children and widows. For fifty-one years, including the difficult ones of World War II, she depended upon God and upon the giving of His people, whether for food for the orphans or for additional buildings. The news of her work spread and many people sent help, but her basic lifestyle remained one of daily dependence upon God and choosing not to worry. She wrote in a book of one very typical experience.[2]

"One day I went to visit one of my Egyptian friends who was ill. I spent the day with her, and she asked me how many children I had [at the orphanage]. I told her and she asked me how much money I had. I told her that I had less than $5 and that I had borrowed $250 from one of my friends."

Lillian's friend was alarmed. Knowing that the orphanage was about to put up a new building, she asked, "Of course you don't start a building until you have some extra money on hand?"

Lillian said, "Oh, we do not wait for money. When we are quite sure that we need a new building, we start if only with fifty cents. By the time the building is finished, it is also paid for."

Lillian tried to reassure her friend, telling her how it had worked in the past. She told her about a recently built two-story dormitory for girls and how they did not owe a cent on it. After several such stories, the woman replied, "Well, Lillian, if I didn't know it was true, I'd say it was all lies!"

Lillian wrote, "As I left that evening her husband gave me $25. The next morning $55 came from America. I paid back part of the $250 which I owed.

"The next afternoon I went up to the nursery. As I looked over the babies' beds, I saw that they were very much in need of some rubber sheeting. Theirs were quite worn out. I said to one of our teachers, 'Oh, if I only had about ten dollars now!' While I was talking, one of the girls called and said, 'Mama, Mrs. D. wants to speak to you on the telephone.' Mrs. D. was a very wealthy Egyptian widow.

"The woman told me that she would like to visit the orphanage, and in a short time two cars drove up. One car was full of oranges for the children, and she gave each child one as they passed by in line. As they left she handed me $150."

Lillian went straight to the store and bought new rubber sheeting for the babies' beds, then used the rest to pay on her $250 debt. The next day, $500 arrived from a donor in America—a healthy contribution toward the ongoing building project. She called her worried friend and reported what God had done in a few days.

"Oh, thank God," the woman replied. "I have hardly been able to sleep at night, worrying about you and all those children!"

The Egyptian woman had lost sleep, but Lillian had not. She had chosen not to worry, knowing that God would provide.

Principle #2: Set Right Priorities

We are to seek first the kingdom of God and His righteousness. Whatever is uppermost in our minds will consume most of our energies and time. It will be the basis for making decisions, and it will be what excites us the most. If we are honest, we will admit that money at times has become our number one priority—not God and His kingdom. If the Lord is in His rightful place in our hearts, we will be unimpressed with money. If we have it or if we don't have it, our eyes will still be on the Lord and not on our ledgers. Often the degree of worry we show over money reveals where we have placed our priorities.

Principle #3: Be Diligent and Responsible

Seeking God's kingdom first, however, doesn't mean that we are to be financially irresponsible. We are told to be sure and know the condition of our flocks (Prov. 27:23) and that the diligent will rule (Prov. 12:24). Each person is to be productive and take care of his own needs (1 Thess. 4:11–12; 2 Thess. 3:10).

Remember the fourth of the Ten Commandments. We often focus on only one aspect of it, honoring the Sabbath. But don't forget the other half of that commandment: "Six days you shall labor."

Some feel that work is a curse and that we would be better off if we didn't have to work. I don't believe that. When God told Adam he would have to work to raise grain for his bread, it wasn't altogether a curse. The desire to be productive is planted deep within each of us. Idleness is the real curse. This is why so many healthy older people who are forced to retire die quickly afterward. We need to return to the truths of the Puritan work ethic. We need to work, and work hard. Then God will bless the work of our hands.

The Bible also tells us we are responsible for our family. We are told to take care of our immediate family and our elderly parents (1 Tim. 5:4). How each individual takes care of financial responsibilities will be different because God calls each person uniquely and equips each one individually for his or her calling. But we do not escape responsibility.

Principle #4: Invest Money and See It Grow

Jesus gave us the Parable of the Talents. This parable makes it clear that we have the obligation to do the best we can to make wise investments. Our money is supposed to be used and grow, bringing blessing to many. It is not to be hidden and hoarded. One caution, however: this does not necessarily mean the growth of financial wealth. That can be included, but there are more important questions. Is our character growing? Is the kingdom of Christ on earth growing? Growth is a principle of life. And yes, a company or an investment also can display Christ's grace of life and multiplication.

Principle #5: Be Generous

Every Christian is to be generous. It's part of what changes in our nature when we become new creatures in Christ. When we are converted, we become like our heavenly Father, who is the most generous of all.

The first reason to be generous is to show God our gratitude and love for Him. We can't send checks to heaven, made out to the Lord Jesus. Ever since He ascended into heaven, the only way we can give financially to Him is to give to others. Giving, then, is one form of worship.

One of the most basic ways to give to God is tithing—giving ten percent of your income. By example and direct command, tithing was assumed as normal for every follower of God throughout the Old Testament. Tithing began before the law (Gen. 14:20), and Jesus made it clear that tithing was to continue without neglect (Matt. 23:23).

However, tithing doesn't make us generous. If we give only ten percent, that makes us one percent better than a thief. God's Word shows us He considers that ten percent is His property and anything less is stealing from Him (Mal. 3:8–9 and Lev. 27:30–32). But the tithe is only to be a reminder to us that He owns everything—one hundred percent of every resource. The Lord says the silver and the gold are His (Hag. 2:8) and that the earth and all it contains are His (Ps. 24:1). We don't own anything, according to God's Word. Anything we have is merely on loan from God, and we are responsible to use it wisely for His purposes.

This is why the New Testament pattern of giving goes beyond the tithe. Generosity doesn't even enter into the picture until we go past the Old Testament minimum of the tithe. Sadly, many Christians haven't yet stopped stealing the ten percent that rightfully belongs to God. In fact, most church-goers do not tithe. According to research by John and Sylvia Ronsvalle, although per capita income increased dramatically between 1968 and 1985, the percentage of income church-goers gave decreased—from 3 to 2.8 percent. They project that if that trend continues, soon giving may be as low as 1.94 percent.[3]

The Word of God states that our entire financial situation is being cursed if we are not tithing (Mal. 3:9). Perhaps you are in this situation and don't see how you can survive and pay all of your existing debts if you don't have 100 percent of what little income you have. Let me tell you a story.

A visiting minister had just completed a stirring sermon on the obligation of every Christian to tithe. He stressed how God would show His faithful provision to those who honor Him by tithing. Afterward the pastor of the small, struggling congregation confided to the visiting preacher, "Actually, my wife and I haven't been able to tithe for several years now. We are barely scraping up enough for rent and food as it is!"

The evangelist listened sympathetically. Then he faced his new friend with a challenge. He told him to try tithing for one year, putting ten percent aside first, before any bills were paid or money was spent. "If you ever find yourself short of the money you need, for any reason,"—he paused and scrawled his home phone number on a business card—"just call me. I'll make up the difference, no questions asked."

A year passed and the younger man called the older one with his exciting report. "I haven't had to call you one time this year. Every week, just like you said, we put the ten percent aside first. And we always had enough money. It just came in. I don't know how exactly, but we always had money for our needs."

"Praise God, brother," the evangelist said over the phone. And then came the clincher. "But why were you able to trust me as a backup and not trust God?"

God Himself is the One who promised to bless us if we tithe: "'Test me now in this,' says the LORD of hosts, 'if I will not open for you the windows of heaven, and pour out for you a blessing until it overflows'" (Mal. 3:10 NASB). One minister said that in all his years of ministering to derelicts on skid row, he never met one who was a giver or one who tithed to the Lord.

If New Testament generosity goes beyond the minimum of the tithe, how much do you give? How do you know when to respond to a need and when to save the money to meet your financial responsibilities, including your own family's? The New Testament rule is simple: everything you are and have belongs to God. And like Jesus, you are to ask the Father's direction in everything. Just say, "Here I am, Lord. And here is all my money. What will You have me do?" When you see a need, ask if you are to give and how much. Obey the Lord. New Testament giving is based on total surrender, listening to the Lord and obeying whatever He tells you to do, then trusting Him to do what you cannot do.

SEVEN

God's Practical Economics

THE TWO MEN WERE obviously from the West. Their clothes alone betrayed them as they hurried down a pot-holed street, pausing now and then to consult a scrap of paper, then comparing it with the few landmarks around them. They couldn't ask anyone for directions—if you didn't know the way to where you were going in Sofia, Bulgaria, in 1968, you probably were not supposed to be there.

Finally the two walked into one house, found their way up a dark stairway all the way to an attic apartment, and knocked. A gray-haired woman opened the door cautiously, then quickly gestured for them to come in. A glance around the tiny attic room spoke plainly of her poverty. One bare bulb cast a half-hearted light over the bed, a small table, two chairs, and several strategically placed buckets, ready to catch roof leaks.

The men identified themselves as Jens and Peter, two Danish Christians, then reached into their pockets and pressed Bulgarian money into the woman's hands.

"This is for the needs of the saints here," Jens explained, "especially the wives of the pastors."

"Oh, my dear brothers!" she exclaimed, clasping the bills in her work-gnarled hands, "what an answer to prayer! Especially for the children!" Jens couldn't help but cringe at her outburst, looking over his shoulder. Was her house bugged? He knew that what they were doing was illegal, but they also knew that many pastors in that country were imprisoned, leaving their families with no means of support. Other Christians had been forced into the most menial jobs because of their stand for Christ. And most believers had large families. So the foreigners brought money for food and rent and clothes. This woman could be trusted to get the money where it needed to go.

As Jens and Peter were leaving, the Bulgarian woman protested, "No, you mustn't go yet! Don't leave without accepting my hospitality." The Danes looked around them. How could they take anything from this obviously needy saint? "No, really, we have just eaten. We must be on our way."

She insisted, however, and proudly sat them down at her table. She carefully placed plain glass tumblers before them. Then, from a small cupboard, she brought out her prize offering of hospitality, a small jar of fruit preserves. She poured cold water in the glasses, then offered teaspoons of the precious jam to her visitors. That was all: just glasses of water and teaspoons of jam.

How do you measure generosity? You cannot measure it in mere dollars and cents. Generosity is always based on the proportion of the gift to what the giver owns. This woman, like the widow whom Jesus observed dropping in her two mites, was fabulously generous.

Every year the United States gives away an amount equal to two percent of its gross national product—$90 billion in one recent year.[1] One of the world's richest nations *should* be giving to help meet human needs. However, what is surprising is *which* Americans are giving. According to a 1988 survey by the Washington, D.C.–based Independent Sector, the highest percentage givers are among those with incomes less than $10,000 a year.[2] The Census Bureau found the same thing: families with incomes under $15,000 gave away twice as much in percentage terms as families with incomes over $100,000.[3] While America has had its occasional generous rich, it is still the widows giving their mites who are outdoing the rest with their generosity.

Faith Giving

It was like that during Paul's time. He held up the churches of Macedonia as an example, who in a great ordeal of affliction and deep poverty had an abundance of joy which overflowed in the "wealth of their liberality" (2 Cor. 8:1–5). These people gave beyond their ability, of their own accord, begging Paul for the opportunity to participate in the needs of saints in other countries. These verses in 2 Corinthians 8 show us several aspects of biblical generosity:

- It is never legislated, but entirely voluntary. We retain the right to personal ownership but freely give what we want to share (verse 3; see also Acts 2:43–47).
- It is lavish, not just something that will not be missed (verses 2–3).
- Even though it is beyond our ability and is costly, if we give because the Lord tells us to, there is great joy in the giving—even hilarity (verse 4; see also 2 Cor. 9:7).
- It comes first out of love for the Lord, then love for people (verse 5).

This kind of faith giving will always be rewarded by the Lord. It comes out of a generous heart, and generosity is an attitude that extends into areas other than money. If we are generous in heart, we will be generous with our time, generous with forgiveness, generous with teaching, generous with our influence, generous with our people, generous with any resource which God has given us.

God's Plan for Provision

We have seen in the previous chapter that giving is a form of worshiping God. But God planned some practical results from our generosity, including provision for special categories of people.

The Bible reveals ways by which provision is made for people. Each of us falls into one of these categories:[4]

- The breadwinners
- The poor and needy
- The sent ones
- The manna people

The breadwinners

God told Adam he would earn his bread by the sweat of his brow. This was the first commandment given after the Fall. The breadwinner category includes the majority of people— those who labor to produce goods or services. Most pastors and evangelists are in this class because they provide a service for which they receive payment. This principle—of full-time ministers being worthy of salaries—was endorsed by Jesus (Luke 10:7) and by Paul (1 Cor. 9:7–14 and 1 Tim. 5:17–18).

A young minister recently said his goal was to use wise investments so that he would be ministering free of charge within a couple of years. At first this sounds good. He would be free to take a pastorate where the people could not support him. He could do any ministry he wanted without having to worry about getting help from anyone. I do not question the motives of this young minister, but I do question the wisdom of this plan. It actually circumvents the biblical pattern of people giving to the one who ministers to them.

The poor and needy

The needs of the poor are to be provided through our generosity. Rather than taxing people and redistributing wealth through impersonal government means, the Bible upholds our right to personal ownership but reminds us to give generously to the poor and needy.

The Bible says we will always have poor among us. There are various reasons for this. Some poor people are innocent victims; others are poor because of wrong choices. But in any case, we are not to harden our hearts (Deut. 15:7, 11; 1 John 3:17), make excuses, or send them away empty-handed (James 2:16). Jesus did not tell us to give only to the deserving poor. He did not say, "Give to him who asks of you—unless, of course, he is a welfare cheat or has been unwise in handling his finances." No, He said, "Give to him." Giving is an act of mercy and mercy is never deserved.

> If one of your countrymen becomes poor and is unable to support himself among you, help him as you would an alien or a temporary resident, so he can continue to live among you. (Lev. 25:35)

When I was a young boy in El Centro, California, we lived across the street from the city park. It was hard times, and the park usually had a hundred or so homeless men sleeping there. Often they came to our back door, standing hat in hand and asking respectfully if we could give them something to eat. I never saw my mother turn one away. We had meager fare ourselves, living off the weekly tithes and offerings of the church folk. But Mom would give them something to eat and perhaps lend a man a quilt to keep warm as he slept in the park.

There are many ways to help people, some of which have a more lasting effect. The Bible makes a distinction between the sluggard and the oppressed poor. We are told that, "If a man will not work, he shall not eat" (2 Thess. 3:10). Therefore we should try to enable the poor to become self-supporting. But the most important thing is that we must not harden our hearts or rationalize away our responsibility to do something to help.

The Lord has many promises in the Bible for those who give to the poor. Here are just a few:

- If you give to the poor, it's like making a loan to God (Prov. 19:17).
- If you give, you will increase (Prov. 11:24).
- You will be blessed (Prov. 22:9).
- You will be great (Isa. 58:10).
- You will be prosperous (Prov. 11:25).
- All your needs will be supplied (Phil. 4:19).
- Your Father will repay you (Matt. 6:4).
- You will be delivered in the time of trouble (Ps. 41:1).
- Your barns will be filled with plenty (Prov. 3:10).
- You will not lack (Prov. 28:27).
- You will have treasure in heaven (Matt. 19:21).
- You will know the Lord (Jer. 22:16).
- The people and the ground which God has given you will be blessed (Lev. 26:5).

The Lord Jesus also said that when we stand before Him in judgment, our treatment of the poor will be one of the criteria by which we are judged (Matt. 25:31–46).

The sent ones

Another category of people I call the "sent ones." I use this term instead of "missionaries" because too often we narrowly interpret missionaries as people wearing pith helmets, preaching under the trees to natives in far-off jungle lands. The original root for the word *missionary* means "a sent one."

These people are sent by one group, selflessly, to do something for another group. It could be one sent to the ghettos of

Detroit. Or it could be one who is sent to build a computer data bank in Switzerland to track worldwide progress of the fulfilling of the Great Commission. Or a sent one could take the Gospel to an unreached tribe in the most distant reaches of the Amazon river basin.

The ones who give generously to the sent ones do not personally receive direct benefit. They give out of their love for God and the realization that the lost can scarcely be expected to pay for someone to bring them the Gospel. Romans 10:14–15 says, "How can they hear without someone preaching to them? And how can they preach unless they are sent?" God intends for our generosity to pay for the sent ones to carry the Gospel (3 John 6–8).

The manna people

Some people, for special purposes and callings of God, are directly supported by God. Like the Israelites receiving manna in the wilderness or Elijah being fed by ravens, this kind of direct provision from God is for a short time, in unusual circumstances, or for a dramatic demonstration of His power.

We have seen such instances in Youth With A Mission. While 175 of our workers were in Greece, preparing the mercy ship M/V *Anastasis* to sail, they saw a direct, manna-like provision. One morning, during a time of relative hardship, 8,301 fish jumped onto the beach in front of their lodging. They carefully salted them away and used the provision for many months to supplement their diet. No one could explain why the fish jumped out of the water. Local Greeks, even the oldest of their neighbors, had never seen such a thing happen. And the fish only jumped out in front of where the YWAMers were staying. It seemed to be a manna provision.

A strange incident happened to Reona Peterson, the young woman whose trip to Albania I shared in the first chapter. On another missionary trip, Reona and a friend named Celia were in Edinburgh, due to leave the next day on a ferry for the Hebrides islands. They were short of money and didn't know what to do. Reona and Celia prayed, asking God to provide. But how would He do it within twenty-four hours in this city where they knew no one?

They walked down Princes Street in the crowd of midday pedestrians and stopped at an intersection, waiting for the light to change. Just as Reona stepped off the curb, she happened to look down.

"Look, Celia!" she exclaimed, "There, on my shoe! How did that get there?" She stooped down and pulled off a one pound note, caught in the buckle of one of her shoes. Then she saw another pound note underneath her foot. They looked up and down the street. No one in the crowd turned. Besides, if someone had dropped the money, how did one of the bills get caught in the buckle? There was no wind that day to have blown the money and somehow impaled it on her shoe. It was exactly the amount they needed for their fare and other needs in the Hebrides. The women were sure that somehow the Lord placed that money on top and underneath Reona's shoe.

Why is this rare? Why are these stories so unusual, even hard to believe? After all, God mysteriously fed millions of His people in the desert for forty years, causing food to "materialize" on the ground for them. He put money in a fish's mouth for Peter to find. So why doesn't He do this more often?

There are several reasons why these "manna" occurrences are rare. Usually God uses people to meet the needs of other people. One reason is, He is doing more than meeting physical needs. He is bringing us together in unity through giving. We will see this in greater detail in the next chapter.

Another reason that God usually uses people is, He wants to show us the truth that it is more blessed to give than to receive. He wants us to learn the blessings of generosity. Then we will become like Him. God loves a cheerful giver (2 Cor. 9:7) because He has the same giving heart. True generosity gives freely, with no strings attached, no selfish motives, and no desire to control. A cheerful giver just gives and allows God to refill his cup so that he can give again.

Corrie ten Boom often taught at our Youth With A Mission schools before she died in 1983. I'll never forget her homely illustration of how God would repay the generous. She stood in front of the class of young missionaries-in-training and placed two bottles before them, each filled with sand. One had a narrow mouth and the other had a wide mouth. She picked up and poured from the wide-mouthed jar. The sand quickly poured out onto the table, leaving the jar empty. She then started pouring sand from the narrow-mouthed bottle. The sand trickled out, taking a long time to empty.

"You see students," she said, waiting for the thin line of sand, "this bottle is like some Christians. They give to God, but not so quickly and freely. But look what happens." She finished and began to reverse the process, pouring sand back into each bottle. The wide-mouthed jar was quickly filled, spilling excess over the top. However, it took her a long time to painstakingly refill the narrow-mouthed jar with sand. It had given slowly and now it received just as slowly.

Which bottle are you like?

EIGHT

Missions Support, the Jesus Way

WHY DOESN'T GOD QUICKLY provide all the money we need for His work on earth? Surely He could lead some billionaire who loves Him to write a huge check, financing the completion of the Great Commission. Or He could help someone who loves Him, someone who could be trusted, to stumble across hidden treasure or strike it rich and give it all to the Lord's work. And why doesn't the Lord cause one of His dear ones to win one of those ten million dollar sweepstakes that come in the mail?

Everyone in ministry who has ever struggled in tears, wondering how he could keep going in his calling, must have asked these same questions. One missionary cried out in frustration, "We never have enough money to do what we're supposed to be doing. It's as if God has tied one hand behind my back and then told me to do just as much work. It's just not fair!"

And why do missionaries have to do newsletters? I'm sure every missionary has sometimes chafed at the continual job of writing letters or producing newsletters for the people back home. Most never write back, after all. And a day or two taken out of a month of ministry to do such communication is sorely missed. After all, the laborers are few in God's work, and the pressures of work are great on those few. So why do we have to do the most important job in the world this way?

We need to get God's way of looking at ministry and money firmly in our minds. We are concerned with what work is getting done and getting the money to see that our goals are accomplished. They are, after all, goals for God's work, aren't they?

However, the Lord has a far different bottom line. His primary concern is restoring relationships—between us and Him and between us and each other. This is why He has designed it so that we rely on others for financial support while we do His work.

Jesus modeled this for us. He supported Himself as a carpenter during His early adult years, but during the three years of His full-time ministry He and the disciples had "Joanna the wife of Cuza, the manager of Herod's household; Susanna; and many others ... [who] were helping to support them out of their own means" (Luke 8:3).

As people give to the work of the Lord, many wonderful things happen. A story from New Orleans illustrates some of what God does through our giving. Ten-year-old Lisa earned fifteen dollars at a garage sale. Instead of spending it on candy or toys or clothes, Lisa decided to give it to an urban missionary named Chuck Morris, who was working with YWAM in the inner city. "Use this money for missions," the young girl said, placing the fifteen dollars in his hands.

Realizing what fifteen dollars meant to a ten-year-old, Chuck carefully considered where to invest it for her. Then he thought of David, a man most ten-year-olds would never have the chance to meet. David didn't have a job and had been sleeping in a city park. But Chuck had just led David to the Lord. David wanted to get a job, but he couldn't afford the ID card required in order to work in Louisiana. Chuck decided to use Lisa's fifteen dollars to pay for the ID so that David could gain self-respect by working at a paying job.

Later Chuck sent Lisa a picture of David and a letter explaining how important her fifteen dollars had been to David. Within a few weeks David also wrote Lisa to thank her and to tell her that he had gotten a job. Today Lisa prays regularly for David, knowing that her giving to the Lord has made a difference in one man's life.

This is just one little story among what must be millions of such stories, but it illustrates the bottom line as far as God is concerned in finances. The bottom line on His ledger is relationships. God showed His love by giving—not only did He give His only begotten Son in the most lavish act of generosity in history, but He continually gives to each of us.

The Word of God tells us every good gift comes from our heavenly Father (James 1:17). We in turn show our love back to Him by giving to others. But instead of merely strengthening our love relationship with God, our giving also binds our heart with the recipient of our giving.

Heart-link Giving

Jesus told us that where our treasure is, our heart would be also. When we give our "treasure" to specific people and their ministries, our hearts will be there with them. We will feel responsible to pray for them, like little Lisa in the story from New Orleans. It may be halfway around the world in an area we may never visit, but we will be closer to those people and to what God is doing in that country because of our giving. It is God's way of forging and strengthening relationships.

Also, something important happens to the receiver of a gift. It is humbling when someone gives to you, especially if you know that they have sacrificed to give to you and your work. It makes you want to be careful and not misuse their trust in you. This is important for everyone to experience. Our pride shrinks from being on the receiving end of generous giving when we cannot repay but only thank the person and pray for God to bless him. We would rather be self-sufficient.

Many times I have talked with people who wanted to be missionaries some day when they could pay their own way to go. But the sad thing is, even if a few could manage not to get entangled in debts and find a way to bankroll their own work, they would miss the terrible-but-wonderful, humbling heart-link that occurs when someone puts money in your hand and says that the Lord told him to give it to you.

There is a special bond forever between you and the person who gave to you. You care about him and you pray for him in a different way than you pray for those who have never given to you personally. You will also naturally want to share news with him about your ministry, reporting what his gift has done in the work of the Lord.

All of these things happen because of God's method of our giving to one another in the body of Christ. Because every ministry needs money, He has guaranteed that we will always need each other and will always be working on our relationships. At the same time the ministries' needs will be met, people with jobs in cities and towns will have their personal vision enlarged and will come to see the world as God does—all because of their giving and the reports they get back from their personal representatives "out there." And prayer will go up on all sides, doing the work of spiritual warfare that is necessary for anything to be accomplished. None of this would happen if we didn't depend upon money, and people giving money, to keep the work of God going.

It may not seem possible to struggling missionaries or pastors, but if a giant foundation were to fund their work or some billionaire were to write a huge check, it could be a death knell for their ministry. Missionaries need more than money. They need people backing them up, praying for the extension of God's kingdom, engaging with them in spiritual warfare through giving and intercession.

A 30/30 Plan for Missions Giving

In Africa a young man from Zimbabwe named Archie Guvi approached me with a question.

"Loren, God has called me to be a missionary. But I don't have financial support, and our people haven't been taught to give to missionaries. What can I do?"

I said to him, "Then you must teach them. Doesn't the Bible in their local tongue say to go into all the world and preach the Gospel to every creature?"

When he demurred, saying that he didn't think his poor people could help him go, I asked how much a soft drink costs in Zimbabwe. "Twenty-five cents," he replied.

"Archie," I asked, "do you know twenty-five people who would give you a cola if you went to their home on a hot day and asked them?"

"Oh yes," he replied.

"Would they do it every day—do they know and love you that much?"

"I think so," he answered.

"Just get twenty-five people to agree to each give you the same amount as for one cola every day."

The next time I heard, Archie was a missionary. I should have challenged him to find thirty, but I just said twenty-five. However, this pattern would work anywhere, at any level of need, with one small adjustment. There are around thirty days in each month (not twenty-five).

What if every missionary were to set a goal to get thirty people who would each be responsible for only one day's expenses for him to work for the Lord? He would have thirty people whose hearts were following their treasure, praying for him, believing in him, and backing him up when he needed encouragement.

What if some emergency came up? Some crisis that demanded extra prayer? That missionary could contact his thirty people for prayer, and those thirty would probably have a circle of influence of ten other people. They could each ask ten to pray, meaning three hundred people could quickly be praying for him.

Extend this to a missionary organization like YWAM, working to carry the Gospel to every part of the world and so dependent upon our prayer base. We could have from 300,000 to 3,000,000 people praying.

This proposal could solve some common problems, too. I have seen burdened pastors all over the world hearing the plea of yet another missionary. The pastor wants to help, yet he is already having a hard time inspiring his people to give. He is pushing a dead weight up a hill, trying to get his people to care about strangers.

There are other inherent problems with less personal missions giving. I have often seen the disappointment of workers having to return from a missions assignment because their supporting church suddenly had a change of pastor and the new pastor didn't know them or believe in what they were doing. As soon as the church came to a tight spot financially, the missionaries' support was cut off. Or even sadder, churches have split or dissolved, leaving missionaries high and dry.

However, when people are supported through relationships with individuals (even if funds are channeled through the local church), as in the thirty day/thirty people plan, if one supporter dies or goes bankrupt or drops out for some other reason, a missionary only has to fast one day a month until he replaces that supporter! Seriously, it would be easier to replace one than to lose all or a majority of his or her support. But most of all, think of the friendships that develop through this "heart-link with purpose"—reaching the world for Christ.

Benefits of Missions Support, the Jesus Way

Jesus was supported by friends—not by a group or an impersonal fund, just friends. There is nothing unbiblical about impersonal means of missions support. But there are many benefits to having people directly supporting people.

- Those who are giving have the joy of participation in someone's ministry. Heart links are formed between people, not between organizational structures.
- There is direct accountability between the missionary and his or her supporters.
- The giver gains direct and timely knowledge of what is happening in missions through the missionary's regular communication.
- Heart-link giving is not as apt to be affected by recession or hard times.
- It gives every missionary the chance to get the help he or she needs, not just those who are doing more "glamorous" or "exciting" ministry.

The late Dr. Donald McGowan, a missions expert at Fuller Theological Seminary, called for Christians to start thousands of mini missions boards, to be directly involved on a personal basis with one or two missionaries. The reason is clear: there are many disadvantages in the more traditional way, where a church supports a list of missionaries. Often no one in the church actually knows the missionaries on their list. Sometimes it has been eight or ten years since a particular missionary visited there. And since it was only a church meeting, the people didn't get to know the missionary as a person. And often no one reads the missionary newsletters except a very busy church secretary who scans the mail, or perhaps a missions chairman. And these people may have only recently started coming to the church and perhaps have never met the people whose letters come in the mail.

Even pastors who are highly motivated to lead their people to give to missions have a hard task under this system. Some confide that they have to surprise their congregation with a missionary speaker so that they won't stay away from another "dull" missions meeting.

A Norwegian Experiment

One of the most innovative plans I have seen lately has been started by YWAM in Norway. They have begun Go Fellowships, small support groups organized for the purpose of sending out new missionaries. Several features of these groups are:

- Each Go Fellowship group is organized as a support group for one missionary. (They have twenty-eight such groups already in operation in various regions of Norway.)
- Every Go Fellowship group includes people from at least two different congregations, to maximize cooperation in the body of Christ.
- These groups meet once a week to pray for their missionary. Also, they read a letter sent from their missionary that week, as well as news from the national office of YWAM. Once a month, they watch a missions video report, YWAM's *Global Perspective*.
- They pray for the unreached people group to which their missionary is going. Sometimes they begin a Go Fellowship focused on an unreached people even before a missionary is found to send to that group.
- They have a full-time coordinator of the Go Fellowships in the national office for YWAM in Norway. This person's job is to keep the Go Fellowship groups updated on news of world evangelism at all times.

Can you imagine the dynamic of such groups? They plan to increase the numbers of these groups each year until they have one thousand groups and one thousand new missionaries. I'm sure local pastors will find these Go Fellowship people fired up to promote missions in many ways in their local churches. Some will probably take their vacations to visit their missionaries. Many will probably end up as missionaries themselves.

Freedom to Make Mistakes, Freedom to Obey God

Some leaders fear this kind of direct involvement by people in missions giving. There is a certain loss of control over the church members' giving. However, loss of control is part of generosity. Anytime you are generous and give, you lose control.

This was the same test I faced when the Lord led us to form a missionary organization without any salaried people. We do not raise money to put in a centralized fund for staff salaries; therefore, we do not have the ability to simply hire and fire workers.

I have had to allow maximum freedom for our several thousand full-time missionaries worldwide. This has allowed them greater liberty to seek God, get His guidance, and go out and obey Him to the best of their ability. Have they made mistakes? Certainly. But there has also been a natural system of checks and balances, as those with new ideas can actually try them out and see if it was the Lord leading them or just some wild idea born of youthful zeal!

Spiritual leaders must be careful not to control and manipulate Spirit-led, blood-bought servants of the Lord in His vineyard. We Christians need to give with open hands, as servants. We must never seek to give with tight control. Giving with too much control will choke initiative and ultimately can even place us in league with the King of Tyre. Satan's method is to control people through money.

Recently a businessman offered to make up the remainder of the budget for a needy work of God in India—provided he be given the majority vote on their board. That isn't Bible generosity or a servant heart of giving.

What about proper financial accountability for the mini mission boards? This could be handled by having a local church assist the mini mission board by issuing tax receipts and asking the missionary for year-end financial statements. A church may fear doing this, thinking this will drain its own funding base. However, in more than thirty years, I have seen that churches with an openness toward their people giving wherever God leads have their own needs met abundantly. It is a corporate extension of the Bible truth of giving and receiving (Luke 6:38).

As individuals support individuals, churches could do the kind of giving most suited to them, giving to large projects with a clear beginning and end.

Bible Principles for Fund-raising

The Bible teaches many principles regarding fund-raising and missions support, even devoting entire chapters to the subject.[1]

For one thing, the Bible teaches the full-time minister to regard gifts from people as sacred unto the Lord. Just as the gifts given to the Levites in the Old Testament were holy (Lev. 22), so every full-time worker should accept gifts with care and under the fear of God. He should never become dull to the fact that people have sacrificed to give to him.

Another principle we can learn from Scripture is the financial accountability that is expected of anyone who handles money which people have given to the Lord's work. When Paul sent Titus on a fund-raising tour for the needy saints, he also sent along an unnamed brother, who was well tested and diligent, to help with the accounting, as Paul said, "taking precaution that no one should discredit us in our administration of this generous gift; for we have regard for what is honorable, not only in the sight of the Lord, but also in the sight of men" (2 Cor. 8:20–21 NASB). Notice, it wasn't enough to be right before God. It also had to look right to the public.

Some groups have glibly failed to honor designated gifts, not giving them entirely to the project or person for whom they were intended. Not only is this unethical, but in many countries it is against the law. It is not right to make excuses, shifting gifts to where we see a greater need. Perhaps, if circumstances change, it may be necessary to contact givers and ask them what to do about their gifts. But we should always honor designations strictly, putting money where givers wanted their money to be used.

Networks of Prayer and Interdependence

When people give as God leads them in their heart, we will see an abundance for His work. The bottom line with God is not money but relationships. He will use giving partnerships to build a network of prayer and strengthen interdependence among His children. As we give, our treasure will be partly here in this worker and partly there in that one, a little in one particular country and some more in another. Our vision and our sense of excitement in being a part of what God is doing all over the world will grow and grow. We will have a stake in it.

It is strange and wonderful to see God's system of economics at work. In Youth With A Mission there is much giving to meet one another's needs. As I have watched the same money change hands, it has amazed me to see how God can do so much. That's the way it was in Hilo, Hawaii, a number of years ago.

As the leaders of a school of missionaries-in-training in Hilo, we became concerned with the amount of unpaid tuition accumulating. We met as leaders to ask God what He was trying to say to us in this situation.

An idea came to my mind to look up 2 Corinthians 8 and read it. I knew it was about giving for the needs of saints, but when I started to read the passage, verses 14 and 15 stood out to me.

"At the present time your abundance will supply what they need ... then there will be equality, as it is written: 'He who gathered much did not have too much, and he who gathered little did not have too little.'"

I remembered the words of an old preacher, who said that in every group God had already placed the amount of money needed for whatever He led that group to do. And now it seemed God was saying to us that we were to meet the needs of these students—thousands of dollars in unpaid tuition—among our 150 staff and students.

We brought the students and staff together and told them what we felt God had said. First, I asked for those who had outstanding school bills to stand and say specifically how much they needed. Then I asked the group to pray individually, or as married couples, and ask God if they were to give, and if so, the amount and to whom they were to give.

My wife, Darlene, and I prayed silently side by side. After a few minutes I whispered, "What did you get, Dar?"

She said, "I felt God said we were to give one hundred dollars to Tom Hallas."

"But, honey, we were supposed to be praying for the needs of students," I pointed out. "Tom Hallas is on staff." It was unspoken, but my meaning was clear: *You got it wrong—that couldn't have been God speaking to you.* Then I told her I had clear guidance to give fifty dollars to a certain student. I couldn't help spelling it out to her: "We don't have one hundred dollars in our bank account, Dar, but we do have just over fifty dollars."

Heads were still bowed. Some were already moving across the group, money was exchanging hands, people were hugging and laughing softly or crying.

"Well, Loren," Dar said, "maybe this is just between me and God. Maybe I'm supposed to trust God by myself for one hundred dollars to give to Tom."

Then I realized I might be about to miss something. We decided to each go back to the Lord but with the other person's impression. I asked the Lord if we were to give one hundred dollars to Tom, and Dar asked if we were to give fifty dollars to the student. To my surprise, we each felt strongly that both impressions were from God. Sometimes people can have different leadings from God and miss the point: God isn't saying *either/or*, but *both*.

I wrote out a fifty-dollar check and took it to the student whose name I had been given. Then I returned to my seat and we waited to see what God would do. We couldn't give one hundred dollars we didn't have.

Just then Tom Hallas came over, his countenance one large question mark. He stood close and spoke softly, so as not to disturb others who were still praying and seeking to hear God's voice.

"Diane and I," he began, gesturing toward his wife, "uh . . . we've been praying. And we think the Lord has told us to give one hundred dollars to a student." He scratched behind his ear, squinting thoughtfully. "But we don't have any money. Loren, do you think God would do that?"

I grinned. "Yes, I do think God would do that! As a matter of fact, God has told Dar and me to give you one hundred dollars, and we don't have it, either. Let's just wait a minute and see what God does."

"Well," Tom shrugged, "at least I feel better." He went back and sat down.

Next a staff member named Debbie Smith approached Dar and me. She had the same question mark on her face. "Loren, God has told me to give you one hundred dollars but to say it's not for you." She looked embarrassed. "Would God do that?"

"He sure would, Debbie. Stand right there. Don't go away." I went and got Tom and Diane. Then I said to Debbie, "Give me the one hundred dollars." She put it in my hand. I turned to Tom, with Darlene beside me. "Tom, God has told us to give you one hundred dollars." He took it and laughed, then turned to find the student to whom he had felt led to give.

I shook my head in amazement. Why didn't God just tell Debbie to give the one hundred dollars directly to that student? Why did He involve Dar and me, Tom and Diane, and then Debbie? I think it was so that we could see a microcosm of the way God's economics work worldwide. The same money—which Haggai 2:8 says all belongs to God anyway—passes from hand to hand, meeting needs, and allowing us all to participate in the miracle of provision, strengthening our unity and challenging us to obedience.

The body of Christ already has the money needed for every work of the Lord. Dr. David Barrett, editor of the *World Christian Encyclopedia,* has stated that two-thirds of the world's wealth is under the ownership and control of Christians.[2] We don't need more money in the body of Christ. We need to get more money flowing. As we give to one another, individual to individual, church to church, across national and denominational lines, the body of Christ will be drawn closer together and to the Lord.

NINE

Living by Faith in the Nine-to-Five World

A LONG TIME AGO in the history of the Christian Church an idea took root which has done great harm. It is this: there is a secular world and a sacred world. Some people are clergy and handle full-time ministry. That's sacred. Other people live and work in the "real world." They have secular jobs. But they can participate in God's work by supporting those in full-time ministry.

Perhaps you have never thought about how deeply this affects your outlook on your work every day. Like many Christians, maybe you consider your job, at best, as neutral in spiritual terms. Or at worst, it is something a little dirty but which has to be done anyway. You go to church on Sunday, and perhaps midweek, to get a spiritual bath before plunging into the filth of the marketplace again.

Great spiritual victories and miracles and financial provision happen but always somewhere else, like on the mission field or to people in full-time ministry. Or maybe they happen to the one in a secular job if he takes time out to do something sacred, like sharing his faith with a fellow employee. Then he closes that sacred compartment and enters into the secular box again, where spiritual things don't happen.

Is this reality? I don't believe so. Miracles can happen on the mission field or your regular job. God is anxious to intervene and help you in the performance of your work. But first you need to see His perspective on your work.

If you love Jesus and are serving Him at the place and in the way He has called, you can live by faith and see spiritual victories in a factory, law office, or department store. As I mentioned in a previous chapter, the word *missionary* merely means "sent one." And Jesus said to all His followers, "As the Father has sent me, I am sending you" (John 20:21).

The only question that remains is one of geography and type of work. How did you take up the profession or job you're in? Did you ask the Lord for His vision for your life? Or like many Christians, did you decide that since you weren't "called" to full-time service, this decision was yours to make?

Many have floated into occupations, finding themselves unhappy years later and never satisfied. Instead of their work being fulfilling and joyful as God intended (Deut. 12:18), it's just something to do to keep bread on the table.

God has a calling for every Christian. We *all* must do all to the glory of God. He doesn't divide callings into sacred ones and secular ones. We have done that. He has a job to do, and He wants us all to take part in it. His job is to extend the lordship of Jesus Christ into every part of society and to take His good news to every person on the planet. As the Lord of the Harvest, He will tell us the part of the field where we are to work.

Know Your Calling

Do you have a calling? A sense of destiny? An overall sense of mission to your life? If not, you can get it. Of course, it requires giving up your rights to your status quo. Maybe God wants to move you and your family halfway across the world. Maybe

He wants you to do something different than you are doing. On the other hand, He may want you to stay right where you are. The only way to be led by the Lord of the Harvest is to surrender the decision to Him.

Once you know you are in the right place—the place of God's choosing—doing the thing God has called you to do, then you act as a missionary would act in that place.

How do missionaries act? If they are effective, they seek God in specifics for how to go about their task. They pray and listen to the Lord's inner promptings and move accordingly. When it looks impossible, as long as they have done what God has told them to do, they can trust God to do what they cannot.

It goes back to our definition of faith in chapter two. Faith is hearing God's voice, putting it into action, then trusting Him for whatever you cannot do. That kind of faith works whether you're making widgets on an assembly line or preaching the Gospel to an unreached tribe along the Amazon.

Many Christians wouldn't do anything they consider spiritual, such as teaching a Sunday School lesson, without praying. Yet the same people wouldn't consider praying about something secular at work—like asking what marketing goals to set, how to handle relations with fellow employees, how to make some system work better, or how to solve a computer problem.

Two scientists, Rod Gerhart and Dr. Wil Turner, were working to develop a new microcomputer-controlled instrument as a project for YWAM's University of the Nations (U of N). As they got into the work, they encountered a problem with the computer system that stumped them for several days. No amount of telephone assistance from the manufacturer or methodical experiments on their part could identify the problem. It just wasn't working the way it should.

Because they were facing a serious deadline, they started working nights, sometimes into the wee hours of the morning. One night they paused to take a break. It was around 2:00 AM, and the two men walked out into the warm Hawaiian night, stretching and unkinking their muscles.

Rod looked up at the bright expanse of stars, framed by gently moving palm trees. *Oh, Lord, You know the answer to this. Please help us,* he prayed silently. Just then, the cause— and the solution—popped into Rod's mind. He yelled to Wil, "I know what the problem is! Come on!" The two men headed back into the lab and put Rod's idea to work. Immediately the system was up and running. A short while later, tired but jubilant, the two scientists locked up and headed home for some rest.

Rod acknowledges that skeptics may say the idea finally came to him, just like it would come to an atheist scientist grappling with a problem. Perhaps Robert Schuller is correct when he says that all creative ideas come from God, regardless of the faith of the person who receives them. But Rod and Wil are convinced that God gave them the answer that night.

Not all of our prayer is directed toward God. Sometimes the enemy of our souls, Satan, is involved. At times we need to address him directly in spiritual warfare, commanding him to stop any activity he is stirring up. Perhaps a difficulty at work or with a coworker is not merely natural in origin.

We shouldn't look for demonic activity in everything, but we should be aware that the enemy may be at work. We can deal with him simply and quickly by taking the authority Jesus gave us over him (James 4:7; 1 Pet. 5:8–9). If we have surrendered to God and are doing what He has called us to, then He is committed to our success.

The entrepreneurial spirit is alive and well in my son, David. While in his teens, he started two small businesses: custom car detailing and David and David Video Productions, a partnership with another film student, David Tokios.

When they first began working together, the two Davids committed to pray together before any shooting or editing. They submitted their work to God and resisted any activity of the enemy. And every day their work went smoothly. Except one day.

That day, during hectic production on a film, they forgot to pray. They were in a hurry and went straight to work. That was the day that everything went wrong. Everything that could go wrong with an editing system did. The more problems that cropped up, the more upset they became—first with the equipment, then with each other. Suddenly they realized what was wrong. They stopped and prayed, took a break, then went back to work. The difficulties smoothed out, and they were able to finish the project successfully.

Does God really care if a video project succeeds? Does the enemy care? Both parties are concerned if we have submitted our work to God. It becomes His work then, and God takes care of His business. And because the enemy works against God and His people, he too is at work, seeking destruction.

Later my son David felt he was to take time out from his business and college to attend two YWAM U of N schools—a School of Biblical Studies in Honolulu and a Leadership Training School in Chile. It didn't make much sense because David and David Video Productions had just taken out a large loan. But they obeyed God and trusted Him with the six-month interruption. David Tokios handled the double load, yet during those six months God blessed their business tenfold.

Commit Yourself to Excellence

If the first thing for Christian businesspeople to know is that they *are* missionaries and that they need to have a calling, then the second thing to realize is that the Holy Spirit is committed to their excelling in that calling.

A friend of mine is David Aikman, Senior Correspondent with *Time* magazine. David has headed *Time* bureaus in Beijing, Berlin, and Jerusalem. It is David's belief that a turning point came for Christians in America after the so-called Scopes Monkey Trial in 1925.

Maybe you read about this historical trial between the State of Tennessee, which had enacted a law outlawing the teaching of atheistic evolution in state schools, and Jerome Scopes, a teacher who had defied the ban by teaching atheistic evolution.

Christians were quite concerned about this trial and filled the courtroom every day. Unfortunately, in the heated legal battle and the fervor of the sometimes unruly gallery, Christians came out looking foolish. The evolutionists won the court case. But what was worse were the media reports, which painted Bible-believing Christians as ignorant, unschooled people rejecting "scientific" thought.

According to David Aikman, this, along with changes of thinking in universities and seminaries around the turn of the century, forced Christians into a defensive mode. Until that time, Christians had held influence-making positions in education, in government, in business, and in the arts. But afterward, according to Aikman, many Christians simply withdrew from the competition. We began accepting mediocrity, we became suspicious of education, and we thought of ourselves as inferior.

Is this overstated? What if your daughter were to come and tell you she felt God wanted her to be in the communications field? Could you see her as an anchor person for a TV network or working as an editor for a leading newspaper? Or would you automatically counsel her to look for a job in Christian communications?

Or have you ever said something like this: "Well, for a Christian novel (or movie), it was really pretty good."

This is not to demean Christian communications, but many young people automatically go for jobs in safe environments, unconsciously avoiding the stiffer competition in the world.

I agree with my friend, David Aikman. We need to regain the leadership we have abdicated. If we live in a "Christian ghetto," perhaps we have helped build the walls. It will take hard work and dedication, but Christians should be able to succeed in whatever field God calls them to. Whenever we apply ourselves and the giftings He has given us, God adds His part to our endeavor. That is what Isaiah 48:17 (NASB) means when it says, "I am the LORD your God, who teaches you to profit."

Integrity

There are many principles of Scripture which translate directly into the business world. One of the most important is integrity. The Word of God says He hates dishonest scales (Prov. 11:1). The scales were the instrument of merchants. Christians who are moving in integrity will make a mark not only for their businesses, but for the Lord whom they serve. The very way they carry out their work and fulfill their obligations, as well as the quality of their products, will make an impact on their community. They will be a blessing.

The Multiplication Principle

The Lord has built growth into all healthy endeavors. This is the Bible principle of multiplication at work. Growth is the natural outcome of following Jesus and using the gifts He has given us with integrity.

In Genesis 1, God said that each would be fruitful and multiply "after its kind." This is the key: is it harmful or a blessing if your endeavor is multiplied "after its kind"? Some people are multiplying a mess. But if you base your business on God's word—if it has a Christian motive and methods—it can be a prototype to be duplicated all over the world, bringing blessing to many. And what is a Christian motive for business? Every business should have at its center people who love God with all their heart, people who want to glorify Christ and serve others in some way.

Serving God and Men

Another important consideration for success is the principle of servanthood. Jesus called us to become servants. This is a vital part of the Christian's life, whether serving in full-time ministry or in the nine-to-five world.

A multibillion-dollar office equipment manufacturer recently learned this principle, taught by Jesus to His disciples. (However, I do not know if the company recognized the Christian source of the principle.) For many years, this organization had been suffering from reduced market share, falling profits, increased customer dissatisfaction, and other problems. Every year management tried to pull the company out of its malaise by setting clear objectives and encouraging their people to work harder. But nothing seemed to work.

Finally they came up with a new approach. They invested an enormous amount of money and three years into retraining everyone in the company—from those in top management down to every single one of their eighty thousand employees. And what was their revolutionary training? Simply put, they were each to determine whom they served. They all asked themselves, "Who is my customer?"

It was easy for the sales people to think in terms of customers. But who were the customers of secretaries, middle management, or executives? It can be said that everyone in an enterprise accepts a task from someone, adds value, and passes it on. Therefore, their customers were the ones they passed their work to. Some groups had to spend weeks and even months just identifying their customers—it wasn't always obvious.

Then through a formalized process, they started asking, "What does my customer need?" After that was answered, a systematic effort was made to determine how to best meet those needs. Finally, customer feedback was required to make sure those needs were being met.

Within a few years the corporation increased efficiency, reduced cost, had greater product quality and output, and had more customer satisfaction. But this daring new concept that they taught their people could be said as simply as this: "Whoever wishes to become great among you shall be your servant" (Matt. 20:26).

If you have the same desire Jesus did, to serve people, you will always be just to your employees. You won't engage in any business practice that forces your workers to put business involvements ahead of God-given priorities like taking care of their families. Your philosophy of loving people and using things, rather than loving things and using people, will flow naturally down to all those working under you.

One Day in Seven

Another important principle for all Christians, including those in the nine-to-five world, is stated in the fourth commandment: we are to keep the Sabbath holy.

Many get nervous when you bring up this topic. They've known strict upbringing with a lot of legalism. It is true that some Christians have gone about as far as the Pharisees in killing the joy of the Sabbath. One person recalled his great-aunt telling a young girl embroidering on Sunday, "You're breaking the Sabbath! In eternity you'll have to pick out those stitches with your nose!"

However, God designed the Sabbath. His principles have much to say to a generation where even young people are burning out from stress.

Sabbath—setting aside work for one day a week—is a constant commitment to trust God with your unfinished work. If paying tithes and living by faith financially is trusting God even when there isn't enough money, then this is its counterpart in carrying your workload. All of us have two precious resources: time and money. Often we do not have the money to do what God is leading us to do, and we constantly do not have the time to complete our task. What do you do when you have too much work to do in too little time? Do you work harder and harder—burning the midnight oil, working every day of the week, sacrificing family, social time, church involvement, exercise, everything—trying to get around to all of it?

Sabbath rest is more than not mowing the lawn on Sunday. Maybe mowing the lawn would be more beneficial and restful, a needed break from the pressures you face at work. Sabbath rest is so important that God included it as one of only ten commandments.

I am indebted to Fraser Haug, a fellow staff member of YWAM in Kona, for some of these insights on the Sabbath.

1. The Lord was the first to observe the Sabbath. He could have kept on creating more species, more plants, more galaxies. But He stopped, saying in effect, "Enough is enough."

2. Another Sabbath that was observed in Israel was that of planting crops for six years and not planting in the seventh year. This created a financial risk, even a risk to the people's existence. Because they did not provide for themselves by the work of their hands, they had to depend upon God in a greater way.

3. There will always be more work than can be done in the amount of time we have. If we are being led of God daily, doing what He shows us and in His priority order, then He will make Himself responsible for what we can't do. That is the spirit of the Sabbath—partnership with the Creator and trust in the Creator.

The key to Sabbath rest is obedience. It's like training a dog to fetch. You throw a stick six times, telling him, "Fetch!" If on the seventh time you throw the stick and say, "Sit!" it is a greater test of his obedience. So we must learn to "sit" or rest, trusting God to complete the work He has started.

There are many other things involved in the observance of Sabbath. These include reflection and evaluation, celebration, sanctification, rest, and refreshment. God has so designed us that if we break the Sabbath law, it will break us. I don't think we should make an absolute in regard to which day of the week the Sabbath is, however. After all, our present calendar is not inspired like the Bible was. It was created in the sixteenth century and has flaws which have to be corrected by leap years.

Certainly, preachers don't have a Sabbath on Sunday. It's a long, hard day of work for them. Also, we need police protection, fire departments, and many other services on Sunday. But those who have to work on Sundays still need to follow God's principle of Sabbath rest. We all must have one day in seven.

During World War II, because of the need for war material, the U.S. Government asked factories to try seven-day work weeks for their employees. They gave several companies contracts to build boats.

One of these companies, Correct Craft, was owned by Walter O. Mellon. Mellon was a Christian, and he refused to put his workers on seven-day shifts. The government responded by threatening to take away his contract, but he persuaded them to give him a little time. He guaranteed that his company would be able to meet their production quotas, even though his competitors were putting their workers on seven-day shifts. After a time it became obvious; the Christian and his company were able to out-produce their competitors, even though they worked only six days a week.

What to Do If You Get Wealthy

Another important principle for Christians in business to remember is this: God is the one who gives you the ability to make money. This may seem obvious, but how quickly we forget it! If in the course of your work you begin to do well, remember the scriptural admonitions to the rich:

> You may say to yourself, "My power and the strength of my hands have produced this wealth for me." But remember the LORD your God, for it is he who gives you the ability to produce wealth. (Deut. 8:17–18).

And,

> Though your riches increase, do not set your heart on them. (Ps. 62:10)

Paul told Timothy to tell the entrepreneurs of his day not to become conceited nor to fix their hope on the *uncertainty* of riches but on God. He also told them to do good, to be rich in good works and generosity (1 Tim. 6:17–19).

All Christians are to be generous and give, but God has given some people special talent to make money so they can give more to God's work. We could call them "Holy Spirit entrepreneurs." Paul referred to these people as having the gift of helping (1 Cor. 12:29) or the gift of giving (Rom. 12:8). One of the many ways God provides is by giving such people ideas that make money.

Some shrink from the idea of wealthy Christians, believing that wealth is unjust. They think that one man's being rich must cause another to be poor. But I believe that ideas are the only limit to wealth. Control of natural resources used to be a guarantee of a nation's wealth, but this is contradicted by Japan, Singapore, Hong Kong, and Korea. These countries have very few natural resources, yet they have prospered. And look at the creation of tiny microchips—made from worthless sand— which is doing so much to make people rich in our day.[1]

If God gives us the power to make money, as Christians we should be careful to ask Him how to use that money. We shouldn't give a grudging tip to God in the offering plate. Instead we should have the attitude of a businessman like R. G. LeTourneau, who ended up "tithing" ninety percent of his wealth. His comment was, "It is not a question of how much money I give to God, but how much of His money I keep for myself."

When God blesses us and we find we have more money than we need, that is a time to ask for God's guidance. Ask God:

- What should I do with this extra money?
- Is there someone I should give it to?
- Should I set it aside and wait for You to show me how to invest it in Your kingdom?

Another reason for businesspeople to maintain generous giving is that they are operating in a world dominated by the King of Tyre. As we have already seen in an earlier chapter, Satan himself is heavily involved in the area of commerce. It is perhaps the area of his greatest activity. Jesus came to redeem commerce and trade. As we give generously for the glory of God, especially to something like missions, which gives us no direct benefit, we are destroying the works of the devil in the world. We are driving back the King of Tyre and rampant greed by moving in the opposite spirit of generosity.

God is looking for open channels He can trust, to bless others through them and their giving. But if they get sticky fingers, God may stop the flow.

A New Kind of Missionary

We need a whole new approach to business. We need people who will seek God and follow His will in their nine-to-five jobs. We need people whose first allegiance is to God and His kingdom, who see their jobs as part of the overall task of bringing Jesus' lordship to the entire earth.

Recently I met just such a person. I can't name him because of the sensitivity of his situation. But he sensed God's call to missions and went to a country where there are many restrictions on preaching the Gospel. There he founded an electronics manufacturing plant. In a few years his business has grown to employ hundreds.

As he has allowed God to spark his imagination, he has invented some unique electronic gadgets. For instance, he showed me something that was a little thicker than a credit card. A talking tract containing a thirty-minute Gospel message recorded on a microchip, it doesn't require any machine to play it. Another invention is a solar-powered, handheld radio, preset to play only one channel—a Christian radio station broadcasting into that predominantly non-Christian region. Not all of his inventions are for evangelism purposes, of course, but these particularly interested me.

Another of his ideas was to alternate Christians with non-Christians on his assembly lines, making it easier for believers to witness during the workday.

Is my friend a missionary? Not in the traditional sense, sent out by a mission board, with pith helmet and a big Bible. But in every other way he is. We need thousands more like him who will dare to submit to God and allow Him to take care of His own business.

TEN

How to Give

H AS THIS HAPPENED TO YOU? You are sitting in your car at an intersection, in the lane closest to the curb. There standing at the curb is a shabby family—a man, woman, and one child. The man is holding up a sign, "Will work for food." What do you do?

You go home, slump into a chair, and begin sorting through your mail. A bunch of bills, some ad fliers, and two newsletters. One is slick and professional. It looks like someone has underlined key passages for you to read, but as you look closer, that too is printed. The other newsletter is crowded onto every square inch of a foreign aerogramme. Both of these letters ask for money to help with some good cause, like buying Bibles to distribute in Russia or feeding starving people in North Africa. Then you flip open a magazine. There, invariably, is a small brown girl with very large eyes. Just for the cost of your morning coffee break, the magazine ad says, you could feed her regularly.

How do you respond to all of this?

Some have responded by becoming hardened to all appeals. They insulate themselves from the homeless, telling themselves that if they really wanted a job, they could find work to do. Or they merely look the other way. It only takes an effort of will to forget the expression on the face of that man beside the intersection with his sign. Sit in your car and look straight ahead. When will that light change? Find a new station on the radio. Maybe even check to make sure the automatic door lock switch is in the right position.

When we are continually bombarded by need, we become either hardened or overwhelmed. Even if we limit our giving to the church, more needs are presented to us than we can respond to. How do you stay tender to needs and open to the Lord in your giving?

Spirit-led Giving

The only way to remain sane, solvent, and soft in our hearts is to ask God to direct our giving. The first step in learning how to give is to ask God. He promises that His sheep will hear His voice. Decide right now that whenever you are presented with a need, you will ask God both whether you are to give and how much. If He says, "No," then you can trust Him to meet the need some other way.

Sometimes not giving can be a real test of your obedience. Don Price was the leader of a small team working in Zimbabwe (then Rhodesia) back in the 1970s. One of the team was a lanky, blond Norwegian named Bjorn Skjellbotten. One day in early December, Bjorn asked Don to pray with him. Bjorn had been working as a short-term missionary in Africa for one year, but now he had to return to Norway for military service.

"What I want you to pray with me about, Don, is the timing. I know it is right for me to go home, but I don't know when the Lord wants me to go."

So Don bowed and prayed with Bjorn. After prayer, Don suggested that Bjorn could leave at the end of that month, December 31. There was a group of students leaving then on an inexpensive flight with LuxAir, headed for the YWAM school in Switzerland. He could travel with them as far as

Luxembourg, then continue on to Norway. Bjorn felt right about this, too, and Don soon forgot about it in the busyness of normal team activity.

The day before the group was to leave, Bjorn approached Don.

"Do you still feel it's God's will for me to leave tomorrow?" he asked.

"Yes," Don replied, searching his memory, remembering that day they prayed together. "I felt God gave us that date, don't you?"

"Uh . . . yes," the young blond said, pausing.

"Why, what's wrong?"

"Well . . . I don't have the money. I thought that if God said I was to go and told me when to go, He would provide the money for me to travel home. I need two hundred rand for the ticket. I've tried to make reservations, and they've put me on standby, but I still don't have the money!"

Don nodded, masking his surprise. How could he explain that because Bjorn came from a more wealthy country like Norway, he had just assumed that Bjorn had the money to return home? And now it was less than twenty-four hours until the flight left.

"Let's just check with God and see if we heard right," Don suggested. The two prayed together, then waited in silence.

"I still think I'm going to leave tomorrow," Bjorn finally said. Don had to agree—he felt the same impression, though he wished he didn't. Another week could make a big difference. He could speak to some Christian friends on Bjorn's behalf . . . or do something.

But all they had was twenty-four hours. Somehow the Lord would have to provide two hundred rand before morning. "I'll trust God with you," Don said, adding confidence to his voice. "Meet me at the airport tomorrow."

Don was late getting there, busy with last minute details, helping the group leaving for Switzerland. As he walked into the terminal, there was Bjorn's blond head towering over the crowd. As he walked over to him, Don saw his bulging knapsack on the floor beside him.

"So, did your money come in, Bjorn?" Don asked. Bjorn just shook his head, managing a small smile. "No, but I guess the Lord can still give me two hundred rand in the next few minutes, can't He?"

Don hurried to the check-in desk to help the others, who were chatting, laughing, and struggling with heavy bags. It was an effort to hide his concern, which was rapidly turning to panic. This young man was trusting God to come through! Don thought for sure someone would have felt led to give to Bjorn or an unexpected offering would have come in the mail, but nothing had. Now the plane was leaving in a few minutes. How could Don explain to him? He would be responsible for this younger believer having his faith in God's guidance and provision crushed.

Don found a seat in the waiting area and began emptying his pockets, counting out his loose change, as if by some miracle he would have enough to help. There was less than twenty rand. He then called his wife and his secretary over, explained the situation, and asked how much they had. After searching through their purses, they found a few more rand and some cents.

By now the group was lining up to go through passport control on their way to the plane. Some were already disappearing into the restricted access area.

"Don! Don!"

Someone called his name from over the heads of the excited group pressing toward the exit. It was Mike Killen, leaving for training in Switzerland. "This is for your ministry here!" Mike hollered. Don grinned as he saw Mike near the front of the line, waving an envelope. Mike passed it back before heading into the inner recesses of the airport, and the YWAMers in line passed it from hand to hand until it reached Don. *Well, God,*

You waited long enough this time! he thought as he opened the envelope and found a wad of bills. As he quickly counted it, he found it was almost enough to pay for Bjorn's fare.

Then Don heard God's voice speak inside his mind—clearly. Too clearly.

This money is not for him.

His heart sank. Don looked back toward where Bjorn was standing, waiting, looking absently out a window. The line of departing passengers was almost gone. *At least he didn't see the envelope,* Don thought, heavyhearted. And then, *Okay, God. I won't give him this. But, please, do something soon!*

Just then a young girl named Thelma Broodryck approached Don. She was a new volunteer, coming to work with them in Rhodesia. Evidently she had come to the airport to see some friends off to Switzerland. Thelma said, "Don, I have two hundred rand here in traveler's checks. I brought it with me for incidental expenses. But I think the Lord is telling me to give this to that Norwegian boy for his trip home."

Don let out his breath, "Praise God!" He mumbled a hurried thanks, and they ran with the traveler's checks to the exchange center. By the time they came back with the cash, all the group had gone. Bjorn was standing with his back to them, talking to Don's wife, Cecilia, and another friend. Before Don could reach him, he saw the ticket agent call to Bjorn, "Mr. Skjellbotten, there's been a cancellation. You may purchase your ticket now!"

Bjorn lifted his knapsack and walked toward the agent. Don sped up to join him, getting to his side just as the agent asked for Bjorn's money.

Before Bjorn could reply, Don said, "Here it is, sir," shoving the bills at the agent. He barely had time to explain to Bjorn what had happened. Bjorn hugged him, shouldered his bag, and headed for passport control.

Giving without the Strings

The second step in learning how to give is to relinquish your rights to the money. So many confuse good stewardship with the desire to keep controlling the money they give. They will donate, provided they have a say in how their money is spent. Unconsciously they are desiring control over the person or ministry to which they are giving.

While we can designate funds when we give, we should not move into the area of manipulating events or people through our money. If you have obeyed God and given to whom He has directed you to give, then trust Him to lead them in how to use it.

The third thing to learn in giving seems almost a contradiction to what I've just said, but it is important to find out how your money is spent. Accountability for funds given to the Lord's work is biblical and sound and partly your responsibility. Find out how much of your gift goes to the intended ministry and how much is spent on overhead and administration, and even how much of your money is spent to raise more money.

Everyone is different when it comes to giving. Some like to give to people, while others like to give to projects that have a beginning and an end. Some prefer giving to mercy ministries; others want their gifts to go to evangelism. Still others like to contribute to training or communications ministries in order to multiply their gifts.

These preferences are not wrong, but we should all remain open to the Holy Spirit and His guidance. In my opinion, the most natural patterns are for people to give to people and for churches or groups to give to projects that have a beginning and an end.

In Youth With A Mission we have been on the receiving and the giving ends of another phenomenon, Christian organizations giving to other Christian organizations. In my book *Making Jesus Lord*,[1] I shared how we went through a painful and humbling process during our first attempt to buy a large ship for ministry purposes. The Lord impressed us to give away $130,000 to Operation Mobilization for the ship they were in the process of buying for ministry. Then, to our amazement, the Lord led other organizations, such as Last Days Ministries, The 700 Club, 100 Huntley Street, The Billy Graham Evangelistic Association, and David Wilkerson Youth Crusades, to give money from their own ministries to us— large gifts which in turn helped us finally buy our first mercy ship, M/V *Anastasis*.

All of this giving underscored our need for the rest of the body of Christ. If there had been any temptation to think that we were special—that somehow YWAM was just a little better than other missionary organizations or Christian groups—the giving from these other groups silenced any whisper of that notion in our hearts.

Getting God's View

In your giving, avoid the tendency to let some needs be out of sight and out of mind. Everyone feels more concern for their own family, their own neighborhood, and their own country. But the God of the whole earth is always trying to lift us up above our narrow little worlds. His concern and tenderness of heart doesn't stop with our city limits or our national boundaries. Get a good atlas, if you don't have one, and study it. Read the international section of news magazines. Become geographically literate. Find out about the whole world, pray for the whole world, and as God leads you, give to the whole world.

Don't throw out that "junk mail" either. In fact, when it comes to Christian newsletters, I have stopped using that term. It is not junk if it acquaints me with something God is doing with other servants in other parts of His harvest. As much as possible, I need to scan these—or give them to others who can—and remain open to the Lord's leading.

How to Take an Offering

This is probably the most casually done, least thought-out part of worship in most churches. Preachers go to Bible school or seminary to learn how to give good sermons from God's Word. A good portion of their week is spent in study and preparation for that time when they enter the pulpit to preach. Musicians and worship leaders also spend years developing skill and take hours each week preparing to lead worship on Sundays.

But where do people go to learn how to take an offering, and how much time is spent praying about how it should be done each week? The most preparation for the offering is usually the music that is played to keep people's minds occupied while the plates are being passed down the aisles.

However, the Bible has a lot to say about offerings. In fact, there are 356 references to offerings in the Bible! As you read about Bible offerings, you will see that they were events of color, drama, and excitement. The leader first spent time with God and got His guidance, then challenged the people to give. Bible offerings were not sandwiched in between the more "spiritual" parts of the service. They were deeply spiritual and often marked by joyful abandon.

For instance, read in Exodus 25 about the offering for the building of the first tabernacle. Notice that those whose heart moved them were told of the need. And the need was very carefully laid out. Specific amounts of gold, silver, bronze, oil, spices, jewels, and purple and scarlet material were requested, and the people were asked to give to meet those needs.

Moses also asked for skilled workers to donate their labor (Exod. 35:10). As you read in Exodus 35 of the great outpouring of gifts and labor, see what a contrast that is to most offerings today. They couldn't have used a pie-sized offering plate, as we usually use in church services—or worse yet, the cloth bag on a stick, in which you hide your hand while dropping in your gift. (I read once that the offering is significantly smaller when the cloth bag is used.) The children of Israel must have hauled in their offerings on carts and made great heaps of them before the Lord. The offering continued several days, according to Exodus 36:3, until the leaders had to stop the people from bringing more. There was more than enough to do the work of the Lord.

Have you ever seen this in your church? I have never seen such an abundant outpouring of love for God that people had to be restrained from giving. I have, however, seen exuberant giving and have learned a little of God's ways in how to encourage people in such giving.

Leaders Must Give Radically

It begins with the leader and his willingness to listen to God's guidance regarding an offering, and his obedience in declaring it to the people. I'm not saying that every Sunday should have a major offering event, as in this example from Moses' leadership. But there are times of *pioneer giving*, where God is leading a group into a big faith challenge. At these times leaders must hear from the Lord and lead out in radical, more generous giving than usual.

As I mentioned in an earlier chapter, some years ago the Lord led us to purchase a castle in Hurlach, Germany. We had moved into the castle with one thousand workers at the time of the Munich Olympic Games outreach. After the outreach, about one hundred staff and missionaries-in-training were housed in this castle, which was paid off in several large payments. Once, we came up to one of these payments and had very little money in our accounts. Yet we needed around 200,000 Deutsche marks, or about $120,000, in two months.

I called together our small group of leaders at the castle. There were six of us who met in David and Carol Boyd's small apartment adjacent to the castle. We sat around their kitchen table, asking God to show us how He wanted to meet this need.

After waiting in God's presence, I heard God speak in my mind, *Give all that you have, and I will bring in ten times that much from the staff and students tomorrow. Then I will bring in ten times their total from outside of YWAM.*

When I told the others what I was sensing as God's direction, they agreed. Someone said that God wanted us to give radically and that there would be great joy.

John Babcock, who was heading up vehicle maintenance at the time, agreed, saying, "As leaders, we have to go first. My wife and I have been saving all year to go back to the States for our children's college graduations. We believe we are supposed to give that." John then laid a check for several hundred dollars on the table.

The rest of us followed suit, until there was roughly twelve hundred dollars on the table in currency and I.O.U.s.

The next day we presented our staff and students with the need. However, we did not tell them what God had told us as leaders—that our giving would be one-tenth of what they gave. I merely told the group of one hundred young people to be silent before God and ask Him if they were to give and how much they were to give.

After a time of silent waiting, they began to give. When all the money and checks were counted, including gifts of watches and cameras, the offering totaled about ten times what we as leaders had given earlier. During the coming days we received financial and material gifts from other Christians, mostly within Germany. Between these gifts and unexpected revenues, the ten times multiplication was realized, and the obligation was met.

Since that time I have often seen God require a small group of leaders to give 10 percent of what was later given by the larger group. It hasn't always been exactly 10 percent, but the leaders have always had to exercise more aggressive faith. The leaders set the pace. The more sacrificially the leaders give, the more their followers give, even though they don't know what the leaders have done. The Holy Spirit knows what the leaders have done, and He stirs the people according to the leaders obedience. As it says in Judges 5:2 (LB), "Israel's leaders bravely led, the people gladly followed!" The inspiration of a leader's faith is multiplied in the people through the work of the Holy Spirit.

King David showed leadership in giving at another great fund-raising time in the Old Testament. They were gathering finances and materials to build the great temple. Chapter 29 of 1 Chronicles tells us first what David personally gave in gold, silver, bronze, iron, wood, onyx, and jewels; then it enumerates what the people gave, following his sacrificial pattern.

An Offering of Lumber

Sometimes the Lord can lead for a special kind of offering to be made, one which captures the imagination of the people. When I was a boy, my father drove a jeep onto the platform in our church sanctuary, asking the people to buy it for a missionary in Africa. It took a lot of trouble to do that. Dad had to temporarily remove a partition separating the auditorium from a fellowship hall, just to have that dramatic giving experience for our church. But the sight of that sturdy jeep and imagining it in the jungles of Africa impressed me as a boy. It impressed me so much that I decided to give the money I had saved for my first car. And many years later I had the privilege of riding in that very jeep in the West African jungle while on a ministry trip to Benin. Remembering Dad's example and following the prompting of the Lord, I have led some unusual offerings among our workers in YWAM. Once we gave lumber for the building of the missions university in Hawaii. We had great loads of lumber, still unpaid for, loaded onto the campus near the meeting place.

Our people prayed. Then, as they felt led, they each went to select one or more pieces of lumber, initialing the ones they would pay for and even writing scriptural promises or commitments to God on the boards. Their writing would later be covered over, but the messages would still be known to God and to themselves.

Later, when I read some of the messages, I wanted to weep. I thought that someday children who initialed a piece of lumber that evening would attend the university to prepare themselves as missionaries. Just imagine a youth sitting inside a classroom, wondering where his piece of lumber was!

The Loaves and Fishes Offering

Another time, we needed $250,000 to complete a building for the study of science and technology in YWAM's University of the Nations in Hawaii. Twelve of our leaders met, and the Lord directed our attention to the story of the feeding of the five thousand with the five loaves and two fish. We were facing an impossibility not too different from the one which faced the disciples that day. I felt God was saying that we were to respond as the boy did and take our "lunch" to Him to multiply.

So twelve of us leaders prayed and asked God how much we were to give personally, believing He would multiply it in the offering from the larger group. However, this time it was different from the experience in Germany. Many of us didn't have money to give, so we made faith pledges.

Alan and Fay Williams were then part of the leadership of the Kona ministry, and although they didn't have any money at the time, they felt God was telling them to trust Him for one thousand dollars to give. Without mentioning the need to anyone, they "prayed it in." One thousand dollars came through the mail to them from various sources during the next few weeks. Dr. Bruce Thompson, another of our leaders, felt God was telling him to call one person and ask for two thousand dollars, and that's how Bruce gave his portion. The total in gifts and pledges from among our leaders was around twenty-five thousand dollars.

The next day we announced to the several hundred staff and students that we were going to have a loaves and fishes meal and offering. At that time there was a large expanse of lawn between the buildings. As people arrived, we had them sit in groups on mats laid out on the grass. We told them of the need. It got rather quiet when we announced that we expected God to provide $250,000 from among our seven hundred staff and students. But some had excitement in their eyes. Then I read aloud the story of Jesus feeding the five thousand.

After reading the story along with words of exhortation and explanation, our leaders began passing out baskets containing chunks of French bread and fish sticks, along with cups of cold water. As the group ate, each of the several hundred asked God if he should give and how much. Meanwhile our Polynesian singing group, Island Breeze, led in praise and worship.

After passing out bread and fish, the leaders acted as ushers, using the baskets to collect money and I.O.U.s. Then they took these into an office, where a group of bookkeepers were waiting with adding machines.

When Martin Rediger, the head accountant, brought me the first total, I interrupted the singing and announced: "So far $1,200 has been given toward our goal of $250,000!" There was silence among the group sitting on the lawn. Crestfallen silence.

But we continued singing and praising the Lord while a person here and there scribbled on a piece of paper or reached into his pocket for some money. By the time Martin came out with a second total, I was able to announce that $6,000 had been given for the building project.

The entire meal and service took about two hours, with the total gradually growing to $14,000, then $27,000, then $32,000, then $47,000. Then it topped $100,000. For many it wasn't a decision to give what they already had or could expect to give. Numbers of the staff and students felt impressed to give amounts of money that they had no way of knowing how they could get. Like Alan and Fay Williams, they were going to pray their money in.

Finally, as the Hawaiian twilight deepened into evening, a couple from Minnesota made a decision, wrote a figure on a piece of paper, and dropped it into one of the baskets. They had lost their high-school-aged son in an automobile accident earlier that year. He had wanted to serve God in the Pacific islands in an area of science and technology. They decided to give some land that was to have been his inheritance. The value of that land, which they estimated on their piece of paper, added to our present balance, brought the total to the $250,000 needed.

When Martin came and gave us that news, we burst out in applause, praising God for the way He had brought in what was needed.

God's provision is available in every situation if the people involved will obey God. If we listen to the Lord and do what He says to do in offerings, the needs will be met from among the people. God has already placed them there with the right amount to give. But obedience has to come before the miracle.

Throwing Money on a Blanket

Once I was flying into Pittsburgh to speak at a conference. While we were approaching the airport, the Lord spoke in my mind. *I want you to take an offering for a new television station that I want to start in this city.* This came as a complete surprise, for I didn't know anyone was thinking about starting a Christian station there.

Yet it was such a strong impression that after my arrival, I told my hosts about it. Russ Bixler was the chairman of the conference where I was to speak.

When I told Russ the word I had received, he stood and stared at me with his mouth open, stunned. Finally he said, "Loren, I'm starting a TV station, but you should tell this to our whole committee, because some are not convinced that the idea for a station is of God."

Later I met with the group, who agreed that it must be God. They said I could take up the offering. I went to my room and prayed, asking God how I should go about it. He directed me to the story of Gideon, who took up an offering by laying down a garment and asking the people to throw their gold on it. It specifically mentioned gold earrings being given.

Taking this as my pattern, I took a blanket from my hotel room to the conference that night. I told the people what God had shown me, first on the airplane, then in the story from Gideon. I asked them to come and throw their offerings on the blanket.

The auditorium was a large one, with tiers of balconies. When the offering began, people began to stream to the stage and throw money on the blanket. Others in the balconies just leaned over the rails and threw money down to the blanket. It was a time of hilarious praise, with singing and rejoicing as we all obeyed God. Some of the people threw jewelry, making it even more similar to the story of Gideon's offering. But nothing prepared us for the thrill when the leaders totaled the amount thrown onto the blanket. It was twenty-five thousand dollars, almost exactly the amount given in Judges 8:26 (LB).

The television station was eventually purchased. In fact, Russ Bixler reports they now have five stations.

This experience in Pittsburgh was not unique. There have been other, similarly dramatic offerings. There was one at the Capel Bible Conference in England, where people heaped up an offering and then danced in a giant ring-around-the-rosy on the lawn outside the meeting place. At a pastor's conference in Arrowhead Springs, California, we were impressed to follow the example in Acts 4:37 and lay our money "at the apostles feet"—in this case, at the feet of the conference's Bible teachers. The methods have been varied, but they have usually been dramatic and full of action. Offerings in the Bible required movement on the part of the people. They came forward to give. They didn't sit passively and wait for a plate to be passed to them.

If we will all be sensitive to the Holy Spirit and His leading, offerings will become a highlight of our lives. Our giving will be varied, exciting, and exuberant. Often it will be beyond what we can do without God's help. And it will be rewarded. As His Word promises,

> Give, and it will be given to you. A good measure, pressed down, shaken together and running over, will be poured into your lap. For with the measure you use, it will be measured to you. (Luke 6:38)

ELEVEN

Invisible Means of Support

Probably the greatest holdup for people considering missions is the money question. How can you know the money will be there when you need it? What about supporting a family? Will you be able to take care of things like your child going to college or getting braces? Many Christians use a term, "faith missionary," which seems intimidating in itself. You may ask yourself, "What if I don't have enough faith to be a missionary?"

First, realize that if God is calling you into full-time service, He knows all about your needs. He knows how many children you have (or are to have). He cares about your elderly parents with failing health. He even sees your daughter's teeth that need orthodontic care. God is practical. Don't be afraid to obey Him, thinking He is not thinking about all the things you are. He is thinking about them, and about the needs you will have that you don't even know about yet.

This is what we talked about in chapter two—the secret the birds have. Their heavenly Father is responsible for them, so they don't worry. And He is certainly responsible for you and your upkeep.

God has various ways to support those in full-time ministry. Don't try to dictate to the Lord the means by which you will be supported. Some are unable to bear the sacrifice of their pride and rely on the gifts of others. They decide they will only minister if they can pay their own way. Others fall into the trap of spiritual pride, believing that the only way to do God's work is to have Him tell people to give to them without their making their needs known. Still others rely too much on people—they look more to their contacts than to God. If He were to lead them to do otherwise, they would have trouble trusting Him.

The Bible says that faith comes by hearing the Word of God. Whether you are just starting out or have been in ministry for years, listen for God's word to you, and do exactly what He tells you to do in each situation.

Look at the variety of experience in Scripture:

- When Jesus and Peter needed money for taxes, He sent Peter fishing, telling him he would find a coin in a fish's mouth.
- When the widow of a full-time minister was about to lose her sons into slavery because of debt, Elisha told her to go to her neighbors and borrow jars, and start pouring the oil she already had. God multiplied that oil for the rest of her life. She sold it, and she and her sons lived off the income.
- When Elijah was hungry, God told him to do a "fund-raising appeal." However, instead of sending out thousands of letters to potential donors with response envelopes inside, he was told to go to one woman— also desperately needy—and ask her directly.

Which means of support is most biblical? Going fishing? Selling oil? Direct appeals? As you read through the Scriptures, you will be struck by one thing in the way God provided for His full-time servants: variety. The Levites lived off the offerings people brought to God's house. The prophets, who had an itinerant ministry, often relied on spontaneous giving, along with hospitality from their friends. For a period of time the apostle Paul made tents, working "night and day" to support himself while pioneering a work in Thessalonica (1 Thess. 2:9). At other times he took up offerings. Believers with means, such as Lydia, fed and housed him.

Until He was thirty, Jesus lived from His earnings as a carpenter. But when He went into full-time ministry, He lived with people and ate at their table. As we saw in a previous chapter, He had a few close friends who contributed to His needs regularly—the Son of God had missionary supporters (Luke 8:3).

While the story of the coin in the fish's mouth showed He could trust God to meet His needs sovereignly, Jesus also made direct appeals. When He needed transportation for His triumphal entry into Jerusalem, He sent His disciples to ask a certain person for the loan of a colt.

Indeed, the only common element in scriptural accounts of provision is obedience to the will of God. The key to living by invisible means of support is *hearing* His voice and *obeying* what He tells you to do.[1] And beware of the trap of expecting Him to lead you the same way every time. Keep flexible and open to His guidance.

Ask the Lord what steps you are to take. At times He may have you tell others about your needs. Obey Him. At other times He may tell you to keep quiet and only make your needs known to Him. Obey Him. Or He may lead you to make an investment. Or sell something you own. Obey Him. He may even bring a business opportunity your way. Something you produce in ministry may bring financial returns.

Beware of any opportunities which divert you from your full-time calling. But don't rule out creative alternatives either, or try to force the Lord to provide for you in a certain way. All miracles of God's provision start by heeding Mary's advice at the wedding of Cana: "Whatever He says to you, do it."

Karen Lafferty was an established nightclub entertainer when the Lord called her into full-time ministry. She knew there would be potential for making lots of money if she kept doing what she was doing, but she also knew she would be disobeying God. If she quit, where would she get the money to live on?

While attending a Bible study at Calvary Chapel in Southern California, Karen was reminded of Matthew 6:33. The passage struck her with force. Later she picked up a guitar as a tune wove its way among the words in her mind: "Seek ye first the kingdom of God and His righteousness. ..." You would probably recognize the tune Karen heard in her mind. It's the same melody sung now in congregations all over the world. "...And all these things shall be added unto you. Allelu, Alleluia."

Karen quickly wrote down the tune and later sold it to a publisher. Today Karen is a missionary. The royalties from that earlier melody, which has been both recorded and put into sheet music, have continued to be part of Karen's missions support to this day.

A Checklist for Moving Out

1. Is God telling me to do this?

How do you know it is really God speaking? Here are a few brief principles. Remember that any impression can come from one of only four sources: your own mind, the mind of others, the mind of God, and the mind of Satan. It's simple to silence any impressions coming from the devil: command him to be silent in Jesus' name. As it says in James 4:7, resist him and he will run away from you.

And what of your own imagination? Is God telling you to do something, or do you want it so badly that you think it's God but it's really you? In order to hear God, ask Him to help you take every thought captive to obey Christ (2 Cor. 10:5). He can cause your tumult of ideas—including those of other people, past and present—to gradually fade and be silent, and His own voice to be heard clearly in your mind. If you are committed to obeying Him, He will make it clear what you are to do.

Remember also that if God is speaking to you, it will be confirmed. Either through circumstances, through the agreement of others, such as your spiritual leaders, or by some sign, such as Gideon received by setting out fleeces. God is not stingy with confirmation if you are honestly seeking Him and willing to do whatever He tells you to do. Make all your decisions in the presence of God, write them down (Hab. 2:2), then do them.

2. How much will it cost?

Making a projected budget is a very important part of obeying God's leading. Some think that spiritual people are sort of dreamy, that they step out into thin air expecting angels to put something under their feet. This is not the case.

One of the greatest miracles in the Bible started with a projected budget. When Jesus told the disciples to feed the hungry multitude, Philip made a quick computation and said that two hundred denarii, or the equivalent of two hundred men's day wages, wouldn't cover the cost. Jesus didn't rebuke him for figuring that out. There is nothing unspiritual about budgets.

Make a list. What are your anticipated needs? Whether God is leading you into a short-term project or into a career of missions, you need to research the costs and write them down.

As you make your projections, avoid the extremes of penury or extravagance. One young woman, trusting God for finances as she entered missions, asked, "Will the Lord provide money for cosmetics?" If it is a need for you, then it is important to Him too. But on the other hand, we should remind ourselves that He promises to supply our needs, not our "greeds."

3. What do I already have?

Anytime God speaks to you, He takes into account what you already have in your possession. He doesn't move miraculously until you are doing everything in your power to make something happen. The feeding of the five thousand started with the little boy surrendering his lunch. Elisha asked the needy widow, "What do you have in your house?" "Nothing," she replied, "except a little oil" (2 Kings 4:2).

What you already have may seem like nothing, too, but God asks you to give it. Do you have a car to sell? Are you holding onto something for a rainy day? Ask the Lord what to do with what you have. He may want you to sell things, or He may ask you to invest what you have. Again, obedience to His guidance is the key.

Some erroneously think that the only way to obey God is not to own anything. Jesus told the rich young ruler to give away everything he had, but He did not give the same advice to Nicodemus, although he was also a man of means.

In our mission we have often seen God tell people to give away what little they had, *even though they were asking God for money themselves.* Many times, the way to get money is to give money—as long as it is done in obedience to the Lord and not out of greed on your part, or as the result of manipulation on someone else's part.

4. Am I to tell others about my need?

In the earliest years of Youth With A Mission, I felt that our workers should not make their needs known. For years I never mentioned a financial need in YWAM newsletters. I did not believe this was the only scriptural way to run a mission; it was simply the way God was leading us at the time.

Then, in 1971, when we were in the process of buying our first property—a hotel in Switzerland for use as a training center—I felt God impressing me to write a letter to our mailing list of several thousand, telling them how much we were trusting God for and asking them to pray about helping us.

I was surprised at my initial reaction to this leading. It was a struggle to obey God and write that letter. I hadn't realized how much I had prided myself on the fact that we were different from many missionary organizations. We could just trust God to lead people to give to us!

I also wasn't prepared for the reaction of some who received our appeal. One close friend wrote an angry letter, saying, "I thought YWAM didn't believe in making financial appeals!" It was enough to make me go back to the Lord. When I did, I realized that I did hear from Him and I had obeyed Him. These reactions showed how narrow we had become, trying to make sure the Lord continued working in the way He had in the past. And unknowingly we passed on the belief to others that God only works when you don't share your needs.

Our need for the purchase of that hotel was met—in exact figures, to the dollar (or in that case, the Swiss franc), and on the final day it was due. We had obeyed God and shared our need.

Faith is obedience to what God tells you, nothing else. So, ask yourself if you are to make your needs known or not. Remember how Elijah was by the brook Cherith, being supported by God alone? Twice a day the Lord sent ravens with his meals. But then the brook dried up, and God told Elijah to go and make his needs known to a person, a widow in Zarephath.

What if Elijah had said to God, "But Lord, You know I don't tell people my needs! I just tell You, and You feed me. I'm too spiritual to ask people!"

There can be definite reasons for making your needs known or for not making your needs known. Part of it has to do with the stage of your ministry.

In those early years of YWAM, for instance, we had little credibility as a mission. We were thought of as young people going out on our summer vacations to do evangelism. Some feared we would take money that was needed for "regular" missionaries. It took time for the public to see that we were regular missionaries, too! (YWAM presently has seven thousand career missionaries serving around the world.) It also took time for the public to see the value of short-term missions. When we began in the 1960s, short-term missions was a new, radical idea.

For pioneering ventures there is often a time of dramatic, sovereign provision from God. Then, as a ministry or an individual becomes established, more people give and are linked in prayer and understanding. That stage is not any less spiritual than the early days, when more miraculous provisions were often needed.

When the Israelites wandered in the wilderness for forty years, they were given food supernaturally every day except the Sabbath. They gathered twice as much manna on the day before the Sabbath. This happened for forty years, every week without fail. They didn't have to work in a garden or even shop at a supermarket. All they had to do was go outside their tents and pick it up.

Imagine how they felt when they entered the Promised Land and were told, "You will now go to work planting vineyards and farms and eat what you grow." Was eating manna living by faith but planting vineyards not living by faith? Both were, because they were both in obedience to God at different stages in their journey.

Sometimes the Lord may lead you not to speak about your needs in order to dramatically prove His love for you. These instances become landmarks of faith to look back on when the going gets tough.

A young man named Clay Golliher was serving with YWAM in the Philippines a number of years ago. When I came through Manila, Clay happened to be the one who met me at the airport. He was almost breathless with excitement—not like his usual, laid-back self.

"Oh, Loren, I just had a wonderful miracle!" he said. He went on to explain he had been totally broke. He didn't even have money for postage to write his folks back home. He only had a few centavos and needed one more peso to mail a letter. The Lord spoke to him to go ahead and write the letter. He did and went by the post office on his way to meet me at the airport.

"Just as I was walking toward the post office, Loren, I saw something out of the corner of my eye, flying by in the wind. I grabbed it. It was a one peso note!" Clay walked into the post office and mailed his letter.

Bryan Andrews is a pastor of a large church in Brisbane, Australia. He was passing through Kona recently, on his way home after a ministry tour in the U.S. We invited him to stay with us for a few days. We didn't know he was out of money.

One day he went to Magic Sands Beach, not far from our university campus. It's a tumultuous little beach, known for fierce tides and heavy waves. While walking along the line where the water met the sand, Bryan looked down and saw twenty dollars floating in the receding surf.

"It meant so much!" Bryan said. "I could've asked some friends here for some money, but I only asked God. I really wanted to hear from Him."

5. *What do I do to get started?*

So many wait their whole lives, wanting to do big things for God. But they never get started. They wait for God to do something.

I like to ask people, "Have you ever seen a dog chasing a parked car?" Of course not. Mark 16:17 says in the King James Version, "And these signs shall follow them that believe ... " But "signs" can't follow you if you are "parked." You have to get moving, break inertia. Faith is not passive. Paul said, "I press on to take hold of that for which Christ Jesus took hold of me" (Phil. 3:12).

A friend of mine named Sam Sasser was used of the Lord in a revival that moved across the Marshall Islands a number of years ago. Sam went there as a missionary in his early twenties and soon led one of the Marshallese kings to the Lord, as well as large numbers of his people. He baptized hundreds in the blue lagoons of those far-flung islands. But it was often hard for Sam and his wife, Florence, to get the money needed to pioneer a work for God in such a poor country.

One day Sam was "just moping," as he described it. One of his friends was a sixty-three-year-old Marshallese man named Barton Batuna, who had preached in the islands most of his life. That day Batuna came and found Sam.

"What's the matter with you, Sam?" he asked.

Sam looked at the man, whose black, wiry, Melanesian frame was like a coiled spring, all energy. He suddenly felt older than this man who was almost three times his age!

"God has told me to build a Bible school here. I want to call it Calvary Bible Institute." Sam sighed and kicked the coral gravel underneath his feet. "But I don't have the money to build it!"

"How much do you have?" asked Batuna.

"Hardly anything. Just two hundred dollars."

"That isn't going to build a school," the Marshallese preacher said.

Sam squinted at him in the bright Pacific sun. Now he wasn't just depressed; he was annoyed.

"No, it's not. And what's more, I haven't the slightest idea how it's going to get built."

"Well, why worry? Let's use two hundred dollars and go as far as we can on that."

So now it's "we," is it? thought Sam, feeling a little better.

"But Brother Batuna, you don't understand. It's not just getting started on the building. We have no cement, and it would take more than two hundred dollars just to get to Guam to buy cement."

Guam was seventeen hundred miles away by plane but was still the closest place to buy building supplies. There was no such thing as having it delivered. It had to be fetched.

"Where's your faith, man?" challenged Batuna. "You've got two hundred dollars. Let's take that as far as it will take us!"

Sam listened to the older man, though it was certainly against all common sense. Why leave the security of his home base to strike out across the Pacific, take an expensive air flight buying not one air ticket but two—and end up stranded on some island with no place to stay and nothing to eat?

Maybe it was the fact that Rev. Batuna kept saying "us" and "we," but an inner voice won out over mental arguments. Sam went and bought the tickets. His two hundred dollars got them as far as Kwajalein Atoll, the site of almost nothing but a U.S. naval base.

When they disembarked on the hot, sunny island, they had thirty-six cents between them and thirteen hundred miles of ocean separating them from Guam.

They decided to go into the navy snack bar and order one hamburger with their last thirty-six cents. At least they could sit for awhile in air-conditioned comfort.

When the hamburger arrived, they carefully cut it in half, then proceeded to eat it slowly and deliberately. Sam's insides were churning.

What have I done? he asked himself. *I should have stayed home! How will I ever get back home? I can't believe I blew two hundred dollars on two tickets to the middle of nowhere!*

They made their hamburger halves last as long as possible. Every now and then Rev. Batuna reassured his young friend.

"Don't worry! We're going to make it."

Just then a Filipino man approached their table. Sam knew some Filipinos were there, working as civilians for the U.S. Navy. The navy had to import laborers to this desolate place.

"Brothers," he addressed them, "and I know you are my brothers in the Lord." Sam glanced at Rev. Batuna, but he looked bewildered too. Who was this guy? "I've been up in my room praying. I'm from Manila," he said, and told them he was from a large church in that city. "You don't know me, and I don't know you. But God sent me down here to give you this."

The Filipino put a paper sack on the table between the two men.

"I love you both. God bless you!"

Then he walked out. Sam sat, staring after the stranger.

"Well," Batuna looked over the top of his glasses at Sam, "are you going to look in that sack or not?"

Sam grabbed the bag and looked in, taking in his breath sharply. Then carefully he began pulling out neat stacks of American dollars and laying them on the table. They counted it. There was ten thousand dollars, saved by a Filipino laborer working far from his country, given to strangers!

It was enough to get them to Guam, of course, and to buy all the cement plus much of the lumber and roofing materials needed to start the building. Sam learned that day that you have to get moving—you have to break inertia—to obey God. If He tells you to do something, start with whatever you have. He will provide the rest.

You Can Limit God's Provision

When God has spoken to you, go for it! God loves aggressive faith. Set your goals with a combination of individual initiative and God's leading.

In the story of Elisha and the widow with the little bit of oil, the amount of God's provision was limited only by the number of vessels she borrowed from her neighbors.

When God promises you something, it is conditional on your doing your part. Halfhearted human effort can prevent or delay God's word from being fulfilled, or can limit how much He is able to do. So never be halfhearted. Do what He has told you to do, and do it with all your might.

In 1972 we were praying in a small group with some of our young people. We had asked the Lord to speak to us and show us what to pray for.

That day God put it on our hearts to pray for our teams ministering on more than thirteen military bases in Europe. One person was led to pray that the Word of God would be emphasized on the American military bases. I got the impression that we were to ask the Lord for the privilege of distributing

100,000 Bibles on the bases. Still another got the idea to pray that there would be public Bible-reading marathons. Then I thought of contacting Dr. Kenneth Taylor (the editor of The Living Bible).

After we finished praying, I telephoned my friend Brother Andrew in Holland to see if he knew Dr. Taylor. It was perfect timing. Brother Andrew said Ken Taylor was in Europe and that he was scheduled to meet with him in a few days!

I contacted Dr. Taylor, who, I learned, had a change of plans and had to return to the States immediately. But he agreed to meet with me the next day at the Frankfurt Airport. I flew there and explained to him briefly about our prayer meeting and the Bible distribution idea. He told me their organization just happened to have 100,000 Bibles left over from a Billy Graham crusade. If we could guarantee responsible distribution, we could have them free of charge.

Dr. Taylor and the publishers of The Living Bible shipped the Bibles to Germany. There, through arrangements by another friend, Colonel Jim Ammerman (Head Chaplain of the U.S. Army V Corps in Frankfurt), U.S. military trucks received the Bibles and distributed them to our teams at military bases throughout Germany, where we, along with other Christians, began handing them out to the soldiers.

Before it was over, everything we had prayed for in our prayer meeting came about. There were Bible marathons in which God's Word was read over public address systems on bases. We passed out 100,000 Bibles free of charge to whoever committed to read them. Copies were read and left dog-eared in military chapels, barracks, and MP stations all over Europe.

Thousands felt the impact—from privates to generals—and many gave their lives to the Lord. A number of soldiers went out as missionaries after their tours of duty ended. Colonel Ammerman returned to Frankfurt a few years ago and found that some of those same Bibles were being read and soldiers were still finding salvation.

God wants to give us big visions—greater challenges and exploits to do for Him. Today you may be praying for a few hundred dollars to go on a short mission trip. In a few years you may be trusting Him for millions for a ministry project. In every situation, go to God first, get His guidance, then work hard to bring it about.

TWELVE

How to Ask for Money

I READ THE FOLLOWING "typical" missionary newsletter in a Christian magazine from England:[1]

Dear Brother or Sister:

Please excuse the faint print and poor quality of paper of our newsletter. But funds are low as we enter the 98th phase of our project to build the Universal Conversion College. As you know from our previous letter we are aiming for a total sum of 23.5 million pounds. At present, we have just topped the 13.50 pound mark and it's marvelous to see the work growing.

It is a great encouragement when you are living by faith to see how all that is needed is provided. We eat regularly. It's my turn on Tuesdays and Thursdays. And it's amazing how many games and activities can be successfully organized in the dark.

Something occurred to me last night as I lay trying to sleep on the linoleum. Our policy of never asking for financial support is what separates us from those projects which constantly seem to be begging. Some have queried our original prophetic word that predicted the college would be built and the whole of England converted by last Wednesday. They suggest it has fallen a little short of fulfilment. We now believe, however, this is due to a spirit of [stinginess] in some individuals outside the project. We prayed for them last night as we read the story of Ananias and Sapphira by candlelight.

Do you know that story, friend?

Yours sincerely,

I understand the signature on the newsletter was shaky and hard to read. Probably the poor fellow was suffering from rickets as well!

Perhaps it would help us learn how to make financial appeals by first learning how *not* to do it.

God judges all our actions by our motives. Therefore, it is very important to have the right motive in giving, and to appeal to the right motives from potential donors.

How *Not* to Raise Money

1. Don't use guilt to ask for money

While our humorous example from England exaggerates to make its point, we have all read newsletters that sounded something like that. "If you don't help us right now, this program will go off the air and millions will go to hell!" or, "Did you know that for the amount you will spend at a restaurant after church today, a family in Central America could eat for a month?"

Guilt is a poor motivator. The Lord loves a cheerful giver, not a guilty, reluctant one. Since "God did not send his Son into the world to condemn the world," neither should we (John 3:17).

2. Don't make financial appeals on the basis of pity

What is wrong with appealing to the pity of people? There is certainly nothing wrong with having compassion for hurting and suffering people in our world, or for those who remain in spiritual blindness without hope for eternal life. But if you continually arouse people's pity, you run a risk. People become hardened to pity, and it takes ever more stark examples to shock them into pity again. They become pity junkies, only responding to higher and higher doses.

The first overwhelming impression of a visitor to Calcutta, India, is the multitudes of needy. Beggars swarm about you wherever you go. People look up at you with appealing eyes and outstretched palms. However, the second thing to strike you is the lack of reaction of those around these wretches. Middle-class workers in white *dhotis* step over sleeping bodies and scramble past the beggars to climb on buses to get to work. They don't seem to see the suffering anymore.

I realize the dilemma of those doing mercy ministries. They struggle to keep a human face on the poverty and pain of the world. The numbers of starving and dispossessed are so great that they have to find ways to bring these facts down to the personal level and show us what we can do to help.

However, pity alone is not enough. We must be led by God in our giving. We should always communicate to donors in a way that allows them to ask the Lord if they are to meet needs and how. We shouldn't try to get them to respond out of the emotion of the moment.

3. Don't appeal to greed

While the Bible does promise "Give and it shall be given unto you," we should never appeal to donors' greed to get them to give to the Lord's work. This is tempting them to sin! We have all seen abuses of this. "Do you need a better car? Give to our ministry, and God will bless you! You can't out-give God!" Tragically, the ones most susceptible to these appeals are the poor.

God's Word is true, and often He blesses wherever He can, even when those making the appeal are manipulating the public. Often, however, when we give money, He doesn't bless us back with more money. Instead, He blesses us in other ways: with joy and with revelation of Himself, His ways, and His character; with a sense of participation in the furtherance of His kingdom; with peace and contentment in our situations.

4. Don't appeal to fear

In the days before *glasnost* and the crumbling of communist power, this was a common appeal: "The only reason God is keeping our nation free from communism is because we are giving to foreign missions!"

While God does indeed bless a nation that is giving to His work, it is wrong to play upon people's fears to get them to give. What they are saying is, "Are you afraid of foreign hordes sweeping into our land? Then you better give generously in the offering, or who knows what will happen?" Others imply that if you give to God, He will keep your loved ones from sickness, injury, or death.

Again, our motivation for giving to God should come out of our love for Him and for the desire to see His kingdom extended throughout the earth. Besides, such appeals seem to suggest that the Lord is looking for loopholes in our obedience, so that He can bring down terrible things upon our heads. This kind of appeal distorts the character of God. We have a loving heavenly Father who sends gentle rain on the just and the unjust. And even when He has to bring judgment upon a people, He does so with great reluctance and compassion.

5. Don't appeal to donors' pride

This kind of appeal is more often done with people of means. "Give to the building fund and we will place a beautiful plaque in the hallway with your name on it." While it is not wrong to honor those who give, don't influence them to pride, making that the reason for their giving. Jesus said that people who give in order to be honored by men have already received their reward. Only those who give with a pure heart, not caring whether anyone else knows what they have done, are rewarded by the Father (Matt. 6:4).

Doing It Right

So, how should we make our appeals for finances? First, we should keep our priorities right. We should never see people as sources for money but always value them as friends. We must guard our hearts to love people and use money, never the other way around.

Every communication, including one in which we present needs, should have as its goal bringing each individual closer to the Lord and to us in relationship. If you could imagine it as concentric circles, think of the circle farthest from you as being a barely interested acquaintance of yours; or for a group newsletter, the farthest circle could be someone in the public who has shown enough interest in your mission to sign something. The goal with each communication is to try to bring people ever nearer, one circle closer. Those in the circles closest to you can hear your deepest need. These are your most committed intercessors, financial-giving partners, and valued counselors. And ultimately, it should not surprise you if these people end up being called into missions themselves. This means you may lose a financial supporter, but the Lord of the Harvest gains another worker, and you gain a coworker to help finish the Great Commission.

First-time missionaries just starting out often say, "But I don't have anyone to tell about my needs." Some point to the fact that their family members hate appeals for finances and don't even believe in what they are doing. (It is true that some would rather their children be unsaved, and home making money at a good job than doing something "crazy" like going into missions.)

Others say they have no way of getting support because none of their friends are Christians—perhaps the worker has only recently come to know Jesus himself. Or he comes from a church which does not give to missions, or only gives to missionaries of their denomination.

If you are obeying what God is telling you and are in His timing, then He has already placed around you people and resources necessary for you to do His will.

Releasing the Ministry of Giving

A few years ago I was speaking to fifty-five leaders of our mission. I asked them, "How many of you have challenged someone to get involved in the ministry of evangelism by describing a particular need?" Every hand shot up. Then I asked, "How many of you have helped get people with teaching ability to use their gifts in training ministries?" Again, every hand was raised. "Have you ever identified someone with a gift of administration and helped channel that person into an administrative aspect of ministry?" Once more, every hand went up.

I paused just a moment. "And how many of you have identified someone with the gift of giving and have challenged him to become involved in the ministry of giving?" This time only two hands were raised. Two out of fifty-five.

Why this hesitancy? Because we haven't seen that the gift of giving is as spiritual and Holy Spirit–driven as the other gifts listed in Romans 12 and 1 Corinthians 12. The Holy Spirit gift of giving needs to be released in the same degree as the gifts of preaching, healing, serving, teaching, exhorting, leading, and acts of mercy.

Get before the Lord with a piece of paper and ask Him to bring names to your mind. Who has shown confidence in what you are doing? Who loves you and believes in you? You may only have one or two, or you may have several. Then ask what you are to ask them for, and how. By letter? By telephone call? In a visit? Or a letter from your leader or leader-to-be?

Being Commended by Someone Else

An idea I heard recently is having someone else commend you and ask for support on your behalf. Really, this is not new at all. My father, T.C. Cunningham, has raised support for hundreds of missionaries in his lifetime. What was new to me was the idea that scripturally there is added influence when another commends you, instead of your having to commend yourself.

Paul spoke in 2 Corinthians 5:12 of not having to commend oneself. He commended, or gave references for, others, such as Phoebe (Rom. 16:1). Paul did not shrink from commending himself, either, when it was necessary. He set forth his case for financial support in 1 Corinthians 9. In 2 Corinthians 11, he gave his full résumé unashamedly. But somehow, when someone else praises you, he or she is freer to point out the good that you are doing and ask people to help you.

Wally Wenge, a member of our International Council, leads a YWAM ministry called Gleanings for the Hungry, which is helping feed hundreds of thousands of needy people by taking tons of leftover produce in Central California, dehydrating it, and shipping it overseas.

Last year Wally and his wife, Norma, decided to tithe one of their ten annual newsletters. They challenged their donors with another missions need, that of YWAM teams in the Amazon. They didn't say anything about Gleanings' needs in that newsletter. The result was they received approximately their usual amount of donations to send to the Amazon *plus* unasked-for donations for Gleanings double their normal amount!

This principle of one person recommending another is worth considering. If you have a friend or leader committed to your ministry and willing to extend himself on your behalf, he can gather people together to help with your support.

What about Non-Christians?

When considering whom to contact, don't automatically rule out people who are not born-again Christians. Of course, you should be especially sensitive in how you present yourself and your work and pray carefully for the Lord to help you. But if it is true that when someone gives his treasure, his heart gradually goes with his treasure, then an unbeliever can be brought closer to the kingdom of God as he gives to God's work.

Obedience More Important Than Money

When we communicate need, we should always encourage people to obey the Lord in their giving. If we become truly convinced that giving to the Lord is true worship, not just some earthly thing we do to keep the spiritual work going, then we can be free to encourage people to give. Giving is a spiritual ministry. Obedience to God is our goal and is more important than money.

A person recently answered an appeal letter to one of our mission workers, Paul Hawkins, telling him, "I prayed about your need, but the Lord told me I was not to give at this time." Paul immediately wrote this person a warm thank you. We should not only write a thank-you note to people who give to us. If they are obeying God in *not* giving to us, we need to express appreciation as well.

When we share our news and needs with people through regular communication, we are allowing them the opportunity to give to our work as prompted by the Lord. We are extending a great privilege to them—the privilege of being involved in what God is doing somewhere else in the world. We should not be apologetic when we extend that opportunity. Neither should we be hesitant when we realize that the Lord truly does bless those who give.

Another thing to consider is that a newsletter is for news, and only once in a while (or in a small part of the letter) should needs be mentioned, except in a true crisis. Like the Aesop fable where the little boy cried "Wolf! Wolf!" we can make people less sensitive to true needs if we are constantly pleading for money.

A final reminder when making your needs known: remember to seek the Lord's guidance as you do so. Sometimes He may lead you to write one or two personal letters. At other times you may need to travel somewhere to talk to one person. Or you may send out a printed newsletter to several friends, asking them to pray about giving. Keep flexible in each situation.

You Never Outgrow the Need for Guidance

The Lord will guide you not only in whom to contact but in what to say. Remember, He is as committed to your ministry as you are—more so, in fact—and He is also anxious to bless those who give. Don't go into the spiritual work of releasing people into the ministry of giving without asking God's help and guidance.

Is there a price to pay in asking for money? Yes, indeed. You have to humble yourself and let people know you are trusting God to lead some of them to help in what you are doing. You will be vulnerable. You may be scared or embarrassed. Some will turn you down. But if you were to spend the day witnessing for Jesus on the streets, many would turn you down as well. You may be surprised at who gives to you and who does not. Moses said, "Take from among you a contribution to the LORD; whoever is of a willing heart, let him bring it as the LORD's contribution" (Exod. 35:5 NASB). Moses didn't worry about those who didn't have a willing heart, but challenged those who were willing to bring their gift to God. Do as Moses did, obeying God and trusting Him with the results.

THIRTEEN

The Question of Affluence

THE GUESTS EAGERLY CROWDED around the dinner table. Their hostess bustled in and served a typically good meat-and-potatoes New Zealand dinner. But when it was time for dessert and tea, she apologized as she poured the pale drink into each cup.

"I'm sorry the tea is so weak," she explained to her guests. "We make it that way to make it go further. You see, we're living by faith."

Her guests assured her it didn't matter to them. In fact, since they were Americans, they were rather relieved that the tea was not as strong as that New Zealanders usually served! And they certainly appreciated the ministry these people were doing, opening their home to people in need and trusting God for their upkeep week by week. But the irony and humor of her statement hit them later, on their way home.

Does living by faith mean weak tea? Does it mean shoes with rundown heels and cars that will hardly start or that you can hear coming when they're a block away? And which was weak, the tea or the faith?

The question of affluence—particularly for servants of God—is an emotional one. It's hard to separate our feelings from fact. The Bless-Me Christians preach that if you have faith, you will have material wealth. If you are not living in prosperity, it's because you haven't exercised your faith.

The Work-Ethic Christians contend that hard work will result in God's material blessing. They say if you don't have money, it is because you have been lazy. Unfortunately, these people are often long on work and initiative but short on mercy and missions giving.

Poles apart from the views of the Bless-Me Christians and the Work-Ethic Christians are those who cast a jaundiced eye on anyone with material goods. These Wealth-Is-Evil Christians stop just short of communism, tracing all the world's ills back to an uneven distribution of wealth. Any serious Christian, according to them, should give away all but the very necessities. Some of these people almost deify poverty—the less you have, the closer you are to God.

Whatever our opinion, most of us feel a mixture of emotions regarding wealth, especially concerning those in the ministry.

Some friends of mine have been working in YWAM for nearly twenty years, mostly in the United States. Over the years they have owned a succession of used vehicles, most with high maintenance costs, dubious reliability, bad gas mileage, and low trade-in values. One vehicle they'll never forget was a Travel-All, which got only ten miles per gallon and was constantly breaking down.

Then they happened upon a good deal on a used car. Although it was seven years old, it was in excellent condition, got twenty-eight miles per gallon, was reliable, economical on repairs, and cost a lot less than a new, economy-sized American car. It was a Mercedes-Benz. My friends bought it, convinced that this was an excellent way to be good stewards of the Lord's money.

They drove this car and other used Mercedes for several years, each time being able to trade in a car and buy another one for about the same amount, while paying far less on maintenance and fuel than they ever had. They were so grateful for the Lord's provision.

Then they started hearing comments about their Mercedes. One person used the word "opulence," while another asked, "How can a missionary afford a car like that?" One even said, "How can they drive that kind of car when there are people starving in the world?"

If only they could hang a sign on the side of the car, listing its cost, how few repairs it required, and how much it saved on fuel every week. Maybe they could even write on its side, "This car is saving the Lord money!" But they couldn't. They prayed and decided they didn't want to be a stumbling block to anyone. The Mercedes had to go.

They traded it in and bought a minivan, which actually cost more than their used Mercedes. The minivan has ended up costing more in upkeep, too, and is depreciating faster. But no one complains about their wasting the Lord's money anymore.

Where does God stand in all this? Is there a certain line of wealth below which you must stay in order to please Him?

Recently I was blessed in a way that brought this question closer home. A few years ago, after our family had lived in a small apartment on the YWAM campus in Kona for years, we had a big surprise. YWAMers all over the world took part in a special offering and gave us a new car and the down payment on a house.

It was so wonderful, especially because of the love that was poured out on us. The house is lovely, but Darlene remarked after a few weeks, "I keep expecting whoever really lives here to come and find us in their house!"

Then a few months ago a man approached me with an unusual gift. He wanted to give me some money, but I could use it for only one of three things. I could put the money aside for my funeral (which I would probably need soon, according to my friend). Or I could save the money to use for nursing care after my stroke (which he also pointed out could happen at any time). Or I could use the money to build a swimming pool and get regular exercise, preventing the other things from happening!

I realize why my friend made his donation with such a strong designation for its use. He knew it would be hard for me to have a swimming pool, even though in our climate it makes a lot of sense. Other friends gave toward our pool, too, and another dear friend donated his expert labor to construct it. The pool is a constant reminder of God's love, and of the wisdom of my friend.

When the Lord wanted to hold up examples of faith to us, He listed a whole cast of heroes in chapter eleven of Hebrews. Abraham, Isaac, Jacob, Joseph, David, and Solomon are listed, and each of these was a wealthy man. But others are listed in the same chapter as examples of faith. These heroes were tortured, mocked, scourged, imprisoned, afflicted, and even killed, and went about destitute, clad in sheepskins and goatskins, living in caves and holes in the ground.

Paul reminded us that either poverty or riches could be the will of God for us and that we can learn to adapt to either:

I know what it is to be in need, and I know what it is to have plenty. I have learned the secret of being content in any and every situation, whether well fed or hungry, whether living in plenty or in want. I can do everything through him who gives me strength. (Phil. 4:12–13).

I have found it more difficult to have plenty than to be in need. It is far easier to listen to the Lord every day when you are trusting Him for the next meal than when things are easier.

Having money is dangerous, according to the Lord. Jesus said it is hard for the rich man to enter the kingdom of heaven and to watch out for the "deceitfulness of riches." God warned His people, when they were given great and splendid cities and houses full of all good things, to "be careful that you do not forget the LORD" (Deut. 6:12).

The writer of Proverbs put it in balance when he said, "Give me neither poverty nor riches, but give me only my daily bread. Otherwise, I may have too much and disown you and say, 'Who is the LORD?' Or I may become poor and steal, and so dishonor the name of my God" (Prov. 30:8–9).

Where do we draw the line? How much poverty is too much, or how much wealth is dangerous? The line varies widely according to three things:

1. Character. It is not a question of how much I can trust God to give me, but of how much He can trust me with. If we are faithful over little, He can make us faithful over much. However, there are two other factors. Our level of provision is also dependent upon
2. our calling, and
3. the culture in which we are working.

Even if God can trust me and my character, He knows what I need—no more and no less—to fulfill His calling on my life.

Provision can vary widely according to what you are doing and where God has placed you to work for Him. I have a friend who was a minister with a generous Christian organization, making a good salary, driving new cars, and living in a beautiful home in the countryside. After a number of years there, the Lord called him to work in the inner city of Los Angeles.

Overnight he and his family found themselves living in a crime-ridden neighborhood with bars on the windows of their house, buying their food in stores where all the windows were boarded up. Instead of shopping regularly for new clothes, they were giving away much of their money to the people in their church, helping them keep groceries on their tables.

Following several years of that, the Lord again led them to change ministries. They accepted the pastorate of a rather affluent church in the Southwest. While still not extravagant, this pastor and his wife found they were required to go shopping for clothes more often and live in a house that was more like the houses of their people.

In each of these three phases of life, my friends were in the center of God's will—using His resources wisely to minister to the culture where He had placed them.

How much is enough money and how much is too much? You cannot come up with an amount. It depends on your situation, your calling, and the people among whom you are working. Norman Vincent Peale pastored a prestigious congregation in Manhattan for years. Mother Teresa worked among the poorest of the poor in Calcutta, India. Yet how each one dresses, lives, and travels depends on his or her calling.

How can you know when you are living too lavishly? While we cannot give an amount, we can have guidelines.

1. We Should Live Not Far Above nor Far Below Those among Whom We Are Serving

My sister and brother-in-law, Jan and Jim Rogers, described one situation. They were visiting some missionaries in Asia, in a country which had recently been impoverished by political upheavals. Because of that country's economy, many missionaries were living in beautiful homes, far better than they could afford in the United States, yet for an average of sixty dollars a month rent.

One evening Jim and Jan were at one of the missionary's homes with other foreign missionaries, enjoying a time of fellowship. A knock came at the door. It was a senior pastor, a national of that country. "He stood there awkwardly on the front porch," Jan said. "He looked like he didn't dare enter the home. Our host stepped outside with him and quickly took care of his questions before returning to the party. We weren't doing anything wrong that night, but somehow I felt an uneasiness come into the room—almost like guilt."

How do you know if you're living too far above (or below) those among whom you are ministering? Ask yourself this question: *Is this (car, house, lifestyle) helping me or hindering me in winning and discipling people for Jesus?*

2. Beware of Greed

The Bible repeatedly makes this warning, especially to those in full-time ministry. We are told, "Be shepherds of God's flock that is under your care, serving as overseer—not because you must, but because you are willing, as God wants you to be; not greedy for money, but eager to serve; not lording it over those entrusted to you, but being examples to the flock" (1 Pet. 5:2–3). Seeking wealth beyond that which is needed to fulfill God's calling is avarice and is condemned in the Bible.

Two things enrage the public today: when preachers are shown to be living lives of luxury and indulgence, and when politicians are getting rich while in public service. Have you ever asked yourself why this is? I think it is because of our society's collective memory of the Bible. The vast majority would not realize that they got these ideas from the Bible, but they did.

The Lord told His people to choose a leader (or king) who would not multiply horses, nor greatly increase silver and gold for himself, so "that his heart may not be lifted up above his countrymen" (Deut. 17:15–20). Likewise, a spiritual leader should be chosen who is "not a lover of money" (1 Tim. 3:3).

Never use ministry to acquire wealth for yourself. There was a reason the Levites were the only tribe not given real estate. Their inheritance was to be the Lord Himself, not material things (Num. 18:20).

We should avoid letting this world's values become our own. We need to bring our spending power to Jesus and let

Him rule in this area of our lives. If your heart is committed to obeying the Lord, He can speak to you and keep your natural desires from running away with you.

3. Avoid Envy of Others and Be Content

The Bible doesn't tell us to avoid wealth or poverty, but we are told to be content. We are told not to compare our lot with others or covet what they have.

How can we overcome in this area? The antidote to envy is to become absolutely convinced of the justice of God. Do a word study in your Bible on the justice of God. Let this truth penetrate your heart and color everything you see. He is fair, and He will bless you—if not financially in this life, certainly in other ways, and for all of eternity. He never promised that we would have equality of goods and provision in this life, only that we would be provided with what we needed.

4. Keep Giving to the Lord As He Leads You

The Lord's way in Scripture is not to pass laws or taxes and forcibly redistribute wealth equally to all. Nor is it to take vows of poverty—this way you could no longer give. His will is that those who are blessed by Him share it generously, of their own free will. This is His will for you, if He has blessed you with abundance:

> Command those who are rich in this present world not to be arrogant nor to put their hope in wealth, which is so uncertain, but to put their hope in God, who richly provides us with everything for our enjoyment. Command them to do good, to be rich in good deeds, and to be generous and willing to share. In this way they will lay up treasure for themselves as a firm foundation for the coming age, so that they may take hold of the life that is truly life. (1 Tim. 6:17–19)

FOURTEEN

When It Just Doesn't Work

WHAT HAPPENS WHEN YOU hear from the Lord, move out to obey Him, and the money runs out? You find yourself checking the mailbox repeatedly. You try to concentrate on your work, but all you can think of is, "Why isn't God supplying my need! I'm doing what He told me to do! Why isn't this working?"

God is absolutely faithful—He can't be anything else. When He gives His word, He will bring it about. Unless . . .

You see, God's promises are always based on our fulfilling conditions. They are never automatic. Let's look at some questions to ask yourself during those times when it just doesn't work.

1. Do I Love Things More Than I Love God (Materialism)?

You don't have to be a rich miser to be in love with money or material goods. You don't have to be wealthy to be materialistic. It isn't a question of how much you own but how much your possessions own you.

Materialism can creep in subtly, little by little, even in full-time ministry, even in missions. You see the needs of the work, you start focusing on the needs of the work, and finally, the needs become greater than your focus on God. You've become a materialist—and all in the name of ministry.

Matthew 6:24 says that no one can serve two masters. You cannot serve God and money. There are several indications when you have turned, deep in your heart, and started serving money instead of serving God.

Ask yourself:

- When I'm praying or our group is praying, how much time is spent praying about financial needs?
- When meeting with others to plan or review ministry, how much time is spent talking about the budget and how we can get more money?

Whatever is uppermost in your heart will show itself. The Word of God says to seek *first* His kingdom and all other things will be added unto you. It sounds as if Jesus was putting "all other things" almost as an afterthought. *Don't worry about it,* He said. *Just do the work God has led you to do. He will take care of your needs.*

- How do I make decisions? Do I ask God what to do, then how to do it? Or do I look at my foreseeable income, then decide what I should do?

When you truly make Jesus Lord, you will make your decisions in a radically different way than those around you. Multitudes are living for the idol of material goods. No one will think you are weird if you move from one side of the nation to the other in order to get a higher salary, even if it means uprooting your family and leaving behind friends, familiar neighborhoods, and everything you love. But if you tell people you are moving in order to obey God, perhaps taking a cut in pay, or even moving into ministry where you have no guaranteed income, you will certainly be considered peculiar. Some may even accuse you of getting involved in a cult or of becoming mentally unbalanced.

When you threaten people's gods, they are going to feel threatened themselves. Longtime friends of mine, Graham and Treena Kerr, were wealthy and famous when they first came to know the Lord. You probably remember Graham from his TV show *The Galloping Gourmet*. When they were converted, God told them to give everything away, and they did. Millions of dollars. They were the rich young rulers who obeyed.

What was surprising was the criticism they received from Christians because of their obedience. Some charged them with not being good stewards. They said they should have invested it, so they could continue giving more and more to the kingdom of God.

Such responses show where people's real values lie. Like the disciples when the woman broke the expensive alabaster vial of perfume over Jesus' head, they say, "This money could have been better spent!"

We don't hear many sermons against idolatry, yet the Bible speaks about this sin more than any other. Three of the first four Ten Commandments—the first, third, and fourth—deal generally with this sin, and the second commandment deals with it specifically. However, we need a new understanding of idolatry in the church. Idolatry is much more than a pagan bowing down to an image. Idolatry is simply living for something other than God. He alone deserves our final commitment, our ultimate devotion and worship.

So, if you find yourself without money, ask the Lord if He is showing you that money has become too important to you. This is not to make you feel condemned. God doesn't condemn, but He does correct us and call us to repentance. And even in correction He is gentle and forgiving. He loves you and wants to see you living in the way that will make you happy and complete. But He knows that will only come when you put Him first in all areas. Therefore, in love for you, He can withhold money until you set your priorities straight.

2. Have I Missed the Will of God?

This is a very obvious but often overlooked question.

What if the owner of a service station leaves for a long vacation, putting you in charge while he is away. He shows you what to do: pump gas for customers, change their oil, and do simple repairs on their automobiles. However, after he leaves, you get a good idea. Why not open a food service area in the station?

Soon you're busy selling hot dogs and donuts and scooping ice cream cones. The trouble is, you are shorthanded, and people who need service for their cars wait and wait, finally leaving in disgust. While you are selling lots of hot dogs, revenues are down, you can't pay the supplier for the gasoline, and you end up shutting down the gas pumps.

By the time the owner returns, your shortfall has grown, putting you in grave trouble financially. You ask the owner for more capital, to get you out of this trouble, and he refuses. Why? Because he owns the service station and didn't authorize you to sell hot dogs, only gasoline. The owner would not be wise if he were to pay for your presumption, would he?

Neither would God be wise if He simply underwrote all of the wishes and flights of fancy undertaken by people in His name. There is a great difference between *faith* and *presumption*. Faith is based on hearing God's voice and doing what He tells you to do. Presumption may appear to be spiritual on the surface, perhaps something you are "doing for God," but in fact, you have moved out on your own without consulting Him.

3. Am I in Debt?

"Owe nothing to anyone except to love one another" (Rom. 13:8 NASB).

Debt can be the reason you are in financial difficulty. God in His love for you holds up your finances until you set matters straight and learn to live responsibly within His provision for you.

Does this mean that all borrowing is wrong? If we are to owe nothing to anyone, should we ever buy property with a mortgage or make car payments?

There are two extremes when approaching Scripture: one is *legalism* and the other is *liberalism.* The Bible sets out absolute truths, such as the Ten Commandments and the declaration Jesus made that no person could come to God except through Him. Liberalism takes these Bible absolutes and makes them relative truths, saying, yes, Jesus is *a* way to God, but Buddha is *another* way.

Other principles in the Bible are relative truths—principles relative to the setting and culture—things such as the admonition in 1 Corinthians chapter 11 about men not wearing their hair long. Some read this verse and go into legalism, making a relative Bible principle into a Bible absolute. But if God is against men wearing long hair, was He also against Samson, John the Baptist, and all others who took the Nazarite vow?

Similarly, if this admonition to "owe no man" in Romans 13:8 (KJV) is a Bible absolute, why does the Bible say to lend to the poor in Deuteronomy 15:7–8? If the poor person accepts your loan, is he disobeying God?

What God is telling us in Romans 13:8 is to be up-to-date, to be current with our obligations. It is financial wisdom to borrow only what you can reasonably expect to repay, and borrow only to purchase items with equity which can be resold to pay your debt if you are unable to meet your obligation.

In other words, borrow money for a vehicle, but don't fall into the trap of borrowing money for food or other items which are consumed, gambling on your future. I am not saying that you should never use a credit card either. If you can keep current without accumulating debt beyond your ability to pay, you are not disobeying the admonition to owe no man.

There are other applications for this principle of owing no man—other reasons for lack of financial provision from God. You can owe someone because you cheated him, stole from him, or hurt him in some way. You could be owing the government because you cheated on your income tax. And just because these things happened before you were a Christian does not make you exempt from the need to make restitution.

For example, what if I were to steal your car, have it repainted, and begin driving it around? In the meantime I become a Christian. But I'm still driving your car, only it's a different color. You take a closer look one day, and you recognize a small dent on the right rear fender and a nick on the windshield. You confront me: "Hey! That's my car you're driving!" What if I replied, "Oh, my brother, I stole your car before I came to Jesus. But that's under the blood now!"

You would not be likely to let me off with that excuse, and neither would God. Perhaps He is holding back financial provision from you, waiting for you to obey that nudge of conscience and make right an old wrong.

4. Have I Been Tithing?

Malachi chapter three states that we are robbing God if we are not giving one-tenth of our income on a regular basis. If we obey Him and start tithing, God promises in Malachi 3:11 (NASB) to "rebuke the devourer for you, so that it may not destroy the fruits of the ground; nor will your vine in the field cast its grapes." If your finances are being devoured, perhaps you have not been diligently obeying God in this area.

5. Have I Been Generous?

Generosity begins after you have paid your tithes. If you have a serious, chronic lack of funds, it could be you are receiving in the same manner you have been giving—feebly and slowly, instead of freely and promptly, as led by the Holy Spirit. Second Corinthians 9:6 tells us, "Whoever sows sparingly will also reap sparingly."

When you find yourself in need of funds, ask the Lord to show you how you can give. Perhaps He will give you money, asking you to give it away, maybe several times, before He gives you more to meet your own need. Or you may give cherished items away, as led by Him, to break a spirit of greed through spiritual warfare. Only the opposite spirit works against the enemy in any situation. If you pray against the devil and his withholding of funds for God's work, it may be necessary to break that spirit of greed by an act of generosity on your part.

Jose and Rosana Liste are two Argentinean YWAMers who went to start a ministry in Resistencia, a very poor area in their country. When the Listes arrived, they were shocked at the conditions. Poor children came to their door, begging for food, and they shared whatever they had. But they were having trouble feeding their own three children—their family of five was receiving the equivalent of only twenty dollars U.S. committed monthly support.

Argentineans love to barbecue on Sunday. One Sunday in April, the Listes were walking home from church and smelled meat cooking in someone's backyard.

"Daddy," cried one of their children, "I want a barbecue! I want meat!" Her mother, Rosana, began to cry, and Jose felt quite helpless. They were out of money and had almost nothing left to eat in the house.

After they got home, a knock came at their door. It was a nine-year-old boy who had often come begging for food. Now he stood there, along with his two brothers, asking for their help.

What could they do?

Then Rosana thought of the story of the feeding of the five thousand with a boy's lunch. She and Jose searched their cupboards. All they found was four half-kilo packages of lentils (about five pounds). They put them in a pot, then asked someone in the neighborhood to prepare a list of the poorest children. There were thirty-six. Jose and Rosana invited them all to come eat, and somehow God multiplied their lentils, scoop by scoop.

From that point on, they began feeding children daily. Each day has been a miracle, but they haven't missed a day feeding the children for months now. The numbers have increased—they're feeding one hundred children plus some mothers every day—and their committed support has grown some. They now receive sixty dollars support a month. That is far, far less than they need for what they are doing.

When Jose is asked how they do it, he just shrugs and smiles. "I don't know how . . . we just do it!" They ask farmers for produce and go to merchants for leftover goods. Once a hunter gave them some doves; Jose mimics the children licking their fingers over the treat of meat. Every day it's different, but God has never failed to provide for them.

Never assume that because you are in ministry, you are exempt from giving. Every Christian is to give. Giving could be the key to your financial breakthrough.

Also, when you are trusting God for His daily provision, avoid the trap of a poverty mentality. Be generous—pick up the restaurant tab whenever possible. It makes no difference if the recipient of your generosity has an income in six figures. You are a representative of the King of heaven.

6. Have I Been Grateful for God's Provision?

The formation of Christ's character in us is what God considers most important. We focus on our needs, even though He always has the ability to abundantly provide for us. He could do for us like He did for Elijah—have ravens bring us chateaubriand in the wilderness, with angels standing by to serve us, asking, "More sauce, sir?" However, the Lord is more interested in changing us into His likeness than in feeding us. Gratitude for what He has given us already is a great part of our learning His ways and character.

In the Old Testament the Levites ate the offerings that the people brought to the temple, but the offerings were still considered sacred. In Leviticus 22:2, the priests were told, "Treat with respect the *sacred offerings* the Israelites consecrate to me" (emphasis added).

When people today give to the work of the Lord, we also must regard that as sacred and holy. Sometimes that is hard to do, when it is obvious that someone hasn't given his best to the Lord's work.

There was a story told of a preacher who received a bushel of apples from one of his parishioners. When asked afterward how his family enjoyed the apples, the preacher replied, "They were just right! If they had been any better, you wouldn't have given them to us, and if they had been any worse, we couldn't have eaten them!"

Seriously, though, there are times when our gratefulness is tested by the Lord Himself. While pioneering the University of the Nations in Kona, Hawaii, there were times of financial leanness. During one of these times, we ate marlin every day for three months. It was God's provision for us, the gift of some fishermen. You can't imagine how many ways of serving that marlin our cooks dreamed up! There was baked marlin, fried marlin, creamed marlin over rice, marlin lasagna, even marlin tacos and marlin enchiladas. We could readily identify with the Israelites, who grew tired of manna.

Times have changed for us in Kona. There would be something wrong if, fifteen years later, we were still eating marlin—unless that was something God was calling us to for life for some reason. The marlin days were days of pioneering, and the spiritual blessings of those days were true feasts. Our delight became what Jesus was doing among us, how He was speaking and leading, not what we saw on our plates when we sat down to dinner.

7. Have I Been Faithful over the Small Things?

Jesus' Parable of the Talents in Matthew 25 is one of the most important passages of Scripture regarding finances. The two servants who invested their capital wisely were given more. The one who didn't had even his small hoard taken from him. The master said to the profitable servants, "Well done. . . . You have been faithful with a few things; I will put you in charge of many things" (verse 23).

This principle of being faithful over a little before we are given responsibility for much is repeated in many areas of our lives. God in His faithfulness will not subject us to the test of abundant money until we have been faithful with our nickels and dimes. God asks in His word, "Who despises the day of small things?" (Zech. 4:10). We are not to despise small beginnings. We are to be faithful in them. Whatever big projects or goals He has put in our hearts to do, He will not release them until we pass our tests in the day of small things.

I learned the principle of faithfulness over small things in a pointed way while we were trusting the Lord for money to buy our first property in Switzerland.

We had planned a special prayer meeting and an offering among ourselves for the down payment on the hotel. The afternoon before the offering I was in downtown Lausanne, just browsing at the Innovation department store. There my eye fell on some great jogging suits, marked down to the equivalent of only twenty dollars! Every morning I had been jogging in some scruffy old pants. As the Swiss passed me looking sleek in their jogging suits, I longed to get more suitable running gear.

A thought flitted through my mind as I stood in the store: *I better buy one today while I have twenty dollars. God may ask me to give all my money during our prayer time tomorrow!* I hurriedly made my purchase.

There, I thought on my way out of the store, with the bag under my arm, *it's done.* I even went jogging that afternoon to confirm my ownership of the jogging suit.

The next day, I sat at the front of our lecture hall. I had led us into prayer, as usual, then instructed everyone to wait on the Lord and do whatever He told them to do. In the quietness of the room, God spoke into my mind.

"I can't release sixty thousand dollars to you to buy this hotel, Loren."

"But why, God?"

"Because I can't even trust you with twenty dollars."

My heart broke as I saw the stubbornness of my heart. It was my twenty dollars all right, but I had hurriedly spent it just in case God would have told me to give it in the offering. Stricken, I stood and confessed to our staff and students what I had done, then prayed and asked God's forgiveness.

Would God have let me buy that jogging suit if I had asked? Maybe so. But I hadn't been faithful enough to ask Him. In His mercy, however, He forgave me. He also, as I had anticipated, asked Darlene and me to give everything we had in that offering, including all that was in our bank account, and the rental property we owned in California—our nest egg. I mentioned earlier in the book other steps of obedience we took and how the remainder of the sixty thousand dollars came in the mail on the last day of our deadline.

8. Have I Disobeyed Anything God Has Told Me?

In the past, when a train jumped its tracks, the engineers had to pull it backward to the spot where it left the tracks before the train could be set on its way again. They couldn't just lift it with a crane and set it back from where it lay. Sometimes a lack of finances can be God's signal to us that we have gotten off the track somewhere. It's amazing how our pocketbooks can get our attention, even when we ignore the clanging alarms of our conscience. God knows that, and in love and mercy to us sometimes withholds our provision until we seek Him and repent.

Disobedience is linked with unbelief in Scripture. Hebrews 3:18 says the children of Israel were not allowed to enter the Promised Land because of their disobedience. And the next verse, Hebrews 3:19, says, "So we see that they were not able to enter, because of their unbelief." Disobedience naturally leads to unbelief. An atheist is an atheist because he has disobeyed revealed truth in the past. Until he is willing to confess that disobedience and start obeying God, he cannot have faith.

It may be more difficult for us, as Christians, to discern our own unbelief. We may say to ourselves, "Oh, but I believe God. I believe His Word!" But how hard is it for you to have faith to believe Him for something specific, for something to happen—today? To you? Unbelief stemming from disobedience may be your problem.

9. Have I Asked God to Supply My Need?

This almost seems too obvious, doesn't it? But have you asked God to meet your needs? James 4:2 says, "You do not have, because you do not ask God." Many times we assume that God knows all about our needs and just wait for Him to provide. He may be waiting for something as simple as our asking. You don't have to set aside ten days to pray and fast to ask Him, either. Just ask Him.

10. Am I More Interested in Learning What God Is Trying to Teach Me or in Having My Needs Met?

This is major. After more than thirty years of living with invisible means of support, I can tell you that this question isn't easy to answer. I remember my feelings one time particularly. We were in a YWAM group, praying for several thousand dollars for rent on our school facilities. We were desperate. A number of the students were late in paying their school fees; we were already in the position of buying meals for the school one day at a time. And there were no reserves to fall back on.

As we were in prayer, Joy Dawson, who was with us teaching, stood and declared: "God, I ask you *not* to provide the money we need until *every one* of us has learned what You're trying to teach us!" I must admit, at that minute I would have settled for some of our students waiting to learn more about God later in their lives!

It was about 9:00 AM when we began praying. We stayed before God, asking Him what to do. The Holy Spirit began to move, convicting some of areas of disobedience, showing others radical steps of obedience to take. The prayer continued until 1:30 in the afternoon.

Then God directed us to take up an offering among ourselves—even though there were only sixty students and a handful of staff. Among that group, more than three thousand Swiss francs were given (around seven hundred dollars). That, combined with what the Lord brought in from outside the mission, met the need.

That happened twenty-one years ago, yet to this day I still have to press into God when there are financial crises and tell Him, "I *am* more interested in learning what You are trying to teach me than I am in having our needs met!" What God teaches us is built into our character and our knowledge of Him and His ways. These are the treasures in heaven of Matthew 6:20 that we are accumulating. These treasures can never be taken away from us. Millions of years from now in eternity we will still be using principles that God is trying to teach us today.

11. Is There "Sin in the Camp"?

This is a question to ask if you are leading a group or an organization that has been facing unmet need. The phrase "sin in the camp" comes from the story in Joshua 7 of the defeat at Ai because of the sin of one man—Achan. Ai was supposed to have been an easy battle, but they lost thirty-six men. Joshua threw himself down on his face afterward, asking God why He had forsaken them! The great warrior's heart turned to putty as he imagined aloud to God every foreseeable disaster. "Oh, if only we hadn't crossed the Jordan!" he lamented. "Everyone will hear about this and come wipe us out. We are dead meat!"

The Lord told Joshua to get up out of the dirt, that there was sin in the camp. He would point it out to him. Sure enough, by a process of supernatural elimination, it was narrowed down to the right tribe, then the right family, then the right tent, and finally the man, Achan.

If you're a leader, you don't have to hire a detective or launch a suspicion campaign when the Lord shows you that sin in your midst is causing Him to withhold blessing. He will make it clear in His own way.

Often He gets our attention with a "mixed blessing" situation, similar to what Amos described in chapter 4, verse 7, where rain fell on one city and not on another.

At one of our large YWAM centers, where each department of ministry has its own budget, one department fell short month after month. The leaders tried to anticipate the needs better and plan for them. However, this department was not only continually running into red ink but suffered from "bad luck" as well. There were mechanical breakdowns and all kinds of problems.

Finally the leaders prayed and sought the Lord. Then it came out: a staff member admitted that he had gotten involved in an immoral relationship with a young woman. When his sin was dealt with, that department was soon running smoothly and in the black again.

It is important to point out that this question is only appropriate if you are in leadership and a group is suffering financial setbacks that are otherwise unexplainable. Much harm can be done if people suspect sin in others every time a group has financial difficulty.

Also, remember that God's provision for you is not dependent upon others' obedience but upon yours. Even if others are disobedient, if you remain faithful and obedient to God, He will find a way to meet your need.

12. Am I Reaping from Past Sins or Wrong Choices?

One reason for financial difficulties is that you may be reaping from past sins. Even though God forgives us when we confess our sins, many times there are consequences that we continue to reap, sometimes for years. In fifty-four verses of Deuteronomy 28, the Bible lists "curses," or ways in which you reap from sinning. Many of the curses mentioned in that chapter are financial: "Your basket ... the crops of your land, and the calves of your herds ... will be cursed."

These curses are built in. God doesn't have to intervene to bring curses upon you; they happen automatically, as the result of certain actions.

Why does God use such curses? Isn't He a God of love? Yes, He is. It is precisely because of His deep love for us that He builds consequences into sin. He knows that nothing hurts us and others as much as our sinning. When we have to live with the consequences of our sin, reaping their effects even after we have received God's forgiveness, it builds a hatred for sin into us.

As someone once said, law without consequences is only advice. When we suffer consequences, we will not be as likely to sin in that way again.

Another possibility is that you are facing the results of foolish choices, not sinful ones. What do you do? In either case, ask people to pray with you. Such curses or consequences can be lifted, lightened, or shortened through the intercessory prayer of others.

13. Have I Been Working Hard?

A young pastor came to an older one, asking his advice about his financial needs and those of his little church. The older pastor asked him to tell him about a typical week. "Well, I have a small congregation—only five or six adults. First, I prepare my message for Sunday. That takes a few hours. Then I do a little bit of visiting. Usually I end up playing golf and doing other things the rest of the week."

The older minister answered, "You're actually getting paid very well, but God is paying you by the hour!"

In other words, get busy. Working for the Lord implies that you really are working, and working hard. Living with invisible means of support means you should be the most responsible, most hard working of all.

Laziness, and the related sins of gluttony and drunkenness, are roundly condemned in Scripture. Here are a few verses to keep in mind:

- "He who works his land will have abundant food, but the one who chases fantasies will have his fill of poverty" (Prov. 28:19).

- "For [the] drunkards and gluttons become poor, drowsiness clothes them in rags" (Prov. 23:21).
- "If a man will not work, he shall not eat" (2 Thess. 3:10).

God put within everyone a desire to be productive. Of course, there are those who cannot work, and we should show them mercy and give them aid. But we should never encourage irresponsibility. Almost every person can be given useful tasks to do.

14. Have I Touched God's Glory?

This is a Bible term which means taking credit away from the Lord and giving it to yourself.

This was the issue in 1 Chronicles 29:11–12:

Yours, O LORD, is the greatness and the power and the glory and the majesty and the splendor, for everything in heaven and earth is yours. Yours, O LORD, is the kingdom; you are exalted as head over all. Wealth and honor come from you; you are the ruler of all things. In your hands are strength and power to exalt and give strength to all.

There is a danger in success in every avenue of life, including ministry. We can allow a subtle shift of attention away from Jesus and onto ourselves as leaders. Money problems are one of the ways the Lord uses to signal that something is wrong.

15. Have I Been Independent and Proud?

A story was told of a devout believer caught in an advancing flood. He refused to be evacuated. He was determined to prove that God would deliver him. The flood waters rose higher and higher, and the man ended up stranded on the roof of his house, praying for a miracle. Three times rescuers came with a boat, but he sent them away. Finally he was swept away and drowned. When he appeared at heaven's door, he was indignant.

"Lord, why didn't you honor my faith?" he demanded.

The Lord answered, "I sent the boat for you three times, but you wouldn't get in it!"

Often we can be asking God to supply a need but refusing His help when He sends it. Perhaps we have a preconceived idea of how He should meet that need. Maybe we aren't willing to humble ourselves and ask others to help in our ministry. We can say we want to have more faith, but actually what we are saying is, "I don't want to rely on others. I want to be self-sufficient."

Independence is a respected character trait. But this strength can also become a sin. Satan tempted Eve by appealing to her independence. The Serpent promised, "You will be like God!"

God wants us to be dependent upon Him and interdependent upon one another, not independent. If we have trouble with an independent spirit, He can use financial holdups to try to get our attention.

16. Have I Been Looking to People Rather Than God to Supply My Needs?

The Bible calls this relying on the "arm of flesh" (2 Chron. 32:8; see also Jer. 17:5). This can be a gradual change over the years. We start out with bare-bones faith, having no idea where the money is going to come from to support us in ministry. The Lord in His faithfulness uses someone to give to us. As this pattern is repeated, we can gradually move our dependence from God to the person who has given to us. Unconsciously, we may even slip into manipulative communication, "the ministry of hints," or outright begging.

We may not know we have shifted our trust from God to man until something happens to our sources—a faithful supporter loses his job and writes to tell us he can no longer give to us. Or a church which has been giving loses several of its big givers—they move away, or the neighborhood changes. Then we face the fact that we have been trusting people, not God. In fact, the idea of trusting God again sounds pretty scary.

This is the wonderful thing about living the life of faith. We can never get too far from our dependence on the Lord. He can use financial need to get our attention, moving us to rely on Him again.

17. Am I Fearful of the Future?

Many are so bound by fear of the future that they cannot step out and obey God. They refuse His call and stay where they are in disobedience.

Fear of the future is a terrible thing, for it grows. How can you ever know if you have enough insurance, enough savings? Have you invested in the right things? Have you thought of every contingency? This kind of insecurity grows and grows until it becomes a paralyzing bondage.

"Perfect love drives out fear," according to 1 John 4:18. We can turn to Jesus for complete freedom from fear. We can trust Him with our future. Everything else is ultimately insecure. Are you putting your trust in savings? What if the federal programs backing up your savings institution go bankrupt? What if the economies of the world fail?

These are not farfetched notions, by the way. In recent years we have seen meteoric rises and falls of economic fortunes. This is partly due to lightning-fast computerized telecommunications systems that link financial and commercial centers on every continent. A financial "hiccup" can cause worldwide financial panic in minutes. If you put your trust in systems of the world, they will fail you. Yet Jesus is greater than the world that He created, greater than the universe which He is sustaining every second "by His powerful word" (Heb. 1:3).

If you are bound with fear of the future, it can be a reason for financial lack. God's word says, "Do not worry about tomorrow.... Each day has enough trouble of its own" (Matt. 6:34). This is not to say that it is wrong to save or invest for the future. Joseph was called to lead Egypt into a savings program, setting aside 20 percent for the future. Listen to the Lord and do what He tells you to do, even if He tells you to make an omelette from your nest egg and enjoy it today, or give it for someone else's nest!

FIFTEEN

If You Fall Off the Edge

I F YOU ARE LIVING a life of faith, your life is based on knowing who God is. Having faith in someone is based on a knowledge of his character—knowing that he will do what he has said he will do. What is this God like whom you are serving? Who is this Person upon whom you are relying for your daily needs? One of His best descriptions is as a father. He is your father, a good father, the very best father in the universe.

Good fathers provide for their children. Good fathers also answer their children's questions. When something goes wrong, when your money stops coming in, just go to your heavenly Father in prayer and ask Him what is causing the holdup.

In the previous chapter, we gave seventeen reasons for financial holdups. If you find yourself without money, it may be due to one of these. Or something else. Your first step is to ask God to tell you. Proverbs 4:7 (NASB) says, "With all your acquiring, get understanding." Too many fail to do this. They get guidance from God to do something, it doesn't work, and they limp away without stopping to find out why. The next time they feel a challenge to do something, they try to trust

God and press on, but they can't. Unanswered questions rob them of their faith.

Living by faith means you have to know *why* it doesn't work when it doesn't work. Learning to have faith in God means asking questions. God is not intimidated by our questions or our failures. We don't surprise Him with our lack of understanding. He knows us better than we know ourselves. He will answer any honest question and will not be angry because we asked. It is not a sin to bring questions to God.

Job was certainly not afraid to ask God questions. He experienced big financial problems, and added to that was the tragedy of losing all his children and the pain of debilitating illness. The Bible says that despite all this, Job never sinned with his lips. And yet he asked questions of God...plenty of questions...loud questions.

If you have gone through all seventeen points in the previous chapter and still don't know why you have "fallen off the edge" financially, ask God if you are being attacked by Satan. If it is something Satan is doing to you, not something you are responsible for yourself, you can easily withstand him with the authority Jesus has given you as a believer.

Command the devil to withdraw from you, according to James 4:7. Then ask God to show you how to counter Satan's attacks by moving in the opposite spirit. If Satan has moved against you with greed, ask God who you can give to and what to give. If Satan has used fear, stand in faith and love. If he has attacked you with rejection, move in forgiveness and acceptance of others.

What to Do Until the Money Comes

There is one other possibility if you are facing a financial holdup. You may have done everything right. God may have indeed spoken to you, you may have obeyed Him exactly, and yet the money doesn't come in. It may be that God Himself is testing you to see if you will remain faithful to Him in difficulty (see Deut. 8:2).

Testing always requires an element of time. Your financial provision may seem late, but God may have a different time schedule. Wait on Him, realizing that the testing of your faith produces perseverance (James 1:3). Determine that you will not give up and that you will overcome by believing and trusting God.

While you are waiting for God to provide, recount His faithfulness to you from the past. This is one of the best reasons for keeping a diary or journal. If you have done this, go back to your diary and read of all the times you have seen God intervene on your behalf. If you haven't kept a journal, go to a friend or your spouse and ask them to help you recount all that God has done in the past: *Remember when we were totally broke that time, needing to pay our bills, and that unexpected income came, just in time? Remember when our little girl needed surgery and we didn't have medical insurance, and the people in our neighborhood decided to take up money for it?*

They did this in the Old Testament. When facing a battle or other crisis, the leader recalled God's acts to the people. Much space in the Bible is taken up with such recountings. Have you ever wondered why God allowed for so much repetition? Why do we have to have the same events repeated in Nehemiah chapter nine that were told in Exodus chapter fourteen? God is showing us a way to overcome, a way to face our battles and build our faith while waiting for Him to intervene on our behalf.

Thank God for supplying your past needs. Often we only notice God's daily provision when it stops.

While waiting for God to provide, don't blame others for your need. Those who blame others never get the real answers. They also lose the joy of living for the Lord.

Avoid falling into the trap of comparing your lot with that of others, too. One YWAM leader told of a time when he and his family were going through real financial testing. They were in a YWAM training program at the time. They noticed that their fellow students had plenty of money, not only to pay their fees but to go out to eat and enjoy treats that he and his family could not afford.

My friend cried out to God, "Why, Lord? Why do they have so much money and we don't even have the money to buy toothpaste?"

God spoke very gently to him. *You can use salt to brush your teeth.*

If you fall into the habit of comparing your level of provision with someone else's, you could be missing what God is trying to do in your life at a particular time. This friend of mine learned that God was meeting his real needs. He was going through a certain period of his life, a time of learning to rely on God in a new way. Today my friend is in a different stage in his ministry. He is one of a handful of leaders carrying the most responsibility in Youth With A Mission worldwide. He and his family have traveled all over the world, seeing God's generous hand of provision.

What we fail to see when we compare ourselves with others is what stage they're in with God at that moment and what stage we're in. I may be being tested at the moment, but I shouldn't expect everyone around me to be tested at the same time or in the same area. If everyone is faring alike, there is no test. The test comes when we see others driving cars and we only have a bike, or we have to walk.

There are many blessings during times of financial need which cannot come in any other way or time. You can learn strength through times of need. You also learn how to identify with the poor as never before.

Jean-Jacques Rousseau told of a "great princess" just prior to the French Revolution. When she heard that hundreds of thousands of people were rioting in Paris, she asked the reason.

"Madame," she was told, "it is because they have no bread."

"Well," she replied, "let them eat cake!"

Many, like this princess, are so sheltered from needy people that they have trouble understanding them. I don't believe this princess was being arrogant. She had no concept that the poor had neither cake nor anything else to eat.

God can use times of temporary need to sharpen our concern, our mercy, and our empathy for the truly poor of the world—for all the millions of people who know true lack every day of their miserable lives.

Another blessing in times of need is to realize the difference between our true needs and our perceived needs. Like my friend complaining about no toothpaste who learned he could use salt to brush his teeth. When we have little, we can learn to thank God that all our real needs are being met.

You also learn during a time of financial lack the truth of God's Word in Luke 12:15, where it says a man's life does not consist of what he owns. You learn that His joy is greater and is not dependent upon money. Habakkuk learned this lesson centuries ago:

> Even though the fig trees are all destroyed, and there is neither blossom left nor fruit, and though the olive crops all fail, and the fields lie barren; even if the flocks die in the fields and the cattle barns are empty, yet I will rejoice in the LORD; I will be happy in the God of my salvation. (Hab. 3:17–18 LB)

When you don't have money, you can have the excitement of seeing God provide your need in other ways.

Shirley Alman told me of a dramatic example of just how good God can be during a time of hardship. She and her husband, Wedge, live in South America, where he is YWAM's International Ministry Director of the Spanish-speaking world. The incident Shirley shared happened years ago, when they were just out of Bible school, pioneering a Hispanic church in Alamogordo, New Mexico.

One day, Shirley tells, "The cupboards were bare, bare, bare. Bare of everything except a few spices—and they don't cook up very well!" It had been nip and tuck for some time, but that day when there was finally nothing to eat, Shirley sat down at her kitchen table and cried out to God. What would they do? Her children were at school, and Wedge was at work. Wedge would come home hungry from working on the construction of their church. He would need to eat something before going to dig on the foundation again that evening. What would she feed him and their four children?

Then she remembered. God was their employer as they struggled to build this church on the poor side of town. What if she wrote out a grocery list for God to fill?

Shirley made out her list—a long one. She included the ingredients for dinner that night, planning on her family's favorite—a Mexican dinner.

That afternoon Shirley went to a meeting with the women in her church. Afterward she drove several to their homes. One woman invited Shirley inside a moment.

As Shirley walked into the woman's kitchen, her heart skipped a beat. There on the counters were several bulging supermarket bags. For her! A quick glance through the bags confirmed that everything on her list was in there except flour.

Shirley's heart was bursting with joy when she returned to her car to drop the other women off. It was hard to keep quiet, but she knew she must—she didn't want her people to know just how desperate they had been. She drove on, but inside she was asking God, "But what about the flour? I can't make tortillas without flour!"

Just as the last woman got out of the car, she said, "Señora Alman, my mother said to tell you she had ten pounds of flour for you. Would you like to pick it up now?"

"Yes," Shirley said. "I want to pick it up now!"

When she was finally alone in the car, Shirley began to sing and praise God at the top of her voice. All of a sudden, she remembered something.

"Beans! Lord, I forgot to put beans on the list!" Shirley tried to remember the contents of the bags—she didn't think there were any beans.

At home, she began to carefully put away her precious groceries. She reached into the bottom of a bag, and there were the pinto beans. God had remembered them, even if she had forgotten.

These kinds of provision are so personal from God they mean even more than if He gave you the money to spend on your needs. He knows if your family likes Mexican food or not. He knows to remember the beans.

God is not limited in the way He provides. He provided for the children of Israel by making their shoes and clothing last for forty years. Just imagine if He had done that for us. We could have been wearing bell bottom pants and leisure suits for forty years!

A time of financial need restores our sense of trusting in God. God always wants our experience to be based not on what He did for us years and years ago but to be immediate and fresh.

Finally, while waiting on God for financial release, meditate on Psalm 37. This psalm seems to be written especially for someone needing money. It tells us three times "fret not" and to trust in the Lord, rest in Him, and wait patiently for Him. It reminds us not to envy others and says that the prosperity of the wicked is temporary.

According to Psalm 37, if you do your part—dwelling in the land and doing good, cultivating faithfulness, delighting in the Lord, committing your way to Him, and keeping His law in your heart—God promises these things:

- He will give you the desires of your heart.
- He will do what is needed in your life now.
- He will bring out your righteousness.
- He will make a judgment for you.
- You will inherit the land.

- You will delight in abundant prosperity.
- He will judge the wicked for you.
- He will sustain you.
- Your inheritance will be forever.
- You will not be ashamed in evil times.
- Even in famine, you will have abundance.
- You will be gracious and give; you will have the ability to meet others' needs.
- Your steps will be established by God.
- When you fall, you won't fall flat on your face—God will hold your hand.
- You will have enough money in your old age.
- Your descendants will be taken care of and will be a blessing to others.
- You will be preserved by God forever.
- You will utter wisdom and speak justice. (You will learn from God and be able to pass that on to others and help them.)
- You will be protected from danger and condemnation.
- God will exalt you.
- You will see the destruction of the wicked.
- God will deliver you; He will be your strength, your salvation and your help.

That's quite a list, isn't it? Yet those are God's specific promises to you, as you wait for Him to provide.

Is the life of faith worth it? If you have ever experienced it, it truly ruins you for the ordinary. Living the life of faith is like walking on a tightrope. It is an incredible thrill.

In the 1800s, an acrobat named Blondin (Jean-Francois Gravlet) became famous for crossing Niagara Falls by tightrope many times, usually with no safety net.

One day a crowd gathered at the falls to watch his most dangerous attempt yet. He planned to push a wheelbarrow loaded with a heavy sack of cement across the tightrope. With that extra weight, the slightest miscalculation could tip the wheelbarrow and twist him off the wire, plunging him to death in the raging waters 160 feet below.

Thousands watched breathlessly as he made his way across, placing one foot carefully in front of the other, quietly pushing the wheelbarrow across the spray-filled chasm, oblivious to the roar of the water beneath him.

When he made it to the other side, the throng let out its collective breath and cheered. What a feat! After his crossing, Blondin challenged a nearby reporter: "Do you believe I can do anything on a tightrope?"

"Oh yes, Mr. Blondin," said the reporter, "after what I've seen today, I believe it. You can do anything."

"Do you believe, then," said Blondin, "that instead of a sack of cement, I could put a man in this wheelbarrow—a man who has never been on a tightrope before—and wheel him, without a net, safely over to the other side?"

"Oh yes sir, Mr. Blondin," said the reporter, "I believe it."

"Good," said Blondin. "Get in."

The reporter paled and quickly disappeared into the crowd. It's one thing to believe something but quite another to have that kind of faith in someone.

However, one person that day did have that kind of faith in Blondin. This brave volunteer agreed to get into the wheelbarrow and cross the falls with the master acrobat.

As Blondin tipped out the bag of cement and placed his passenger in the barrow, men on both sides of the falls quickly placed bets on the outcome. Then as the crowd cheered, Blondin made his way back across the falls, this time pushing a nervous passenger ahead of him.

It looked like another easy conquest for the daredevil. But when they were halfway across the sixteen-hundred-foot rope, a man with a heavy bet against them crept over and cut one of the guy wires.

Suddenly the tightrope pitched crazily back and forth, the force of the whipping motion gaining in intensity. As Blondin fought to keep his balance, he knew that they were seconds away from death. When the rim of the wheelbarrow came off the wire, they would both be pitched headlong into the churning waters.

Blondin spoke, cutting through the terror of his passenger in the wheelbarrow. "Stand up!" he commanded. "Stand up and grab my shoulders!"

The man sat there paralyzed.

"Let go and stand up! Let go of the wheelbarrow! Do it or die!"

Somehow the man managed to stand up and step out of the swaying wheelbarrow.

"Your arms—put them round my neck! Now your legs—round my waist!" said Blondin.

Again the man obeyed, clinging to Blondin. The empty wheelbarrow fell, disappearing into the frothy turmoil far below. The aerialist stood there, using all his years of experience and every trained muscle to stay on the wire until the pitching subsided a little. Then inch by inch he made his way across, carrying the man like a child. Finally he deposited him on the other side.

That's what it means to live the life of faith. You have to have real confidence in the One who is carrying you across. It is fairly easy to say you believe in God. But are you willing to have Him carry you across a tightrope, high above a roar of water? You can have that experience, you know. You can have the thrill of trusting God and seeing Him meet your needs.

This is what it comes down to, in living by faith. It is faith in God Himself. There is no system or ritual to it. It is faith in a living person, faith that He will help you accomplish the job He has given you to do.

He has big challenges, planned just for you. He wants you to have a major part in the most exciting race of history—the race to take the Gospel to every creature. He wants to see you be the best you can be—for Him, and for your world around you. Take up the challenge. Step out for Him. Trust Him. Dare to live on the edge.

Appendix

The Creation of Wealth and the Alleviation of Poverty

Don Johnson

Just past the break of day, two men stand on a street corner. The taller man is well dressed, impeccably groomed with a leather briefcase tucked tightly under one arm. The second man's clothes are tattered; his lack of socks are made obvious by his ill-fitting trousers. This poor man is weak looking and sad, with lines of frustration and despair clouding his otherwise young-looking face. He shivers in the brisk morning air, strangely shadowed by the tall, confident stranger who hurries past him.

This contrast is often passed unnoticed by the average person; however, at various times, a scene such as this will freeze in our memory, and we are forced to reflect upon it. These contrasts are evident in every part of the world. It exists in developing as well as developed nations, in all international economic systems throughout the world. It is the gap between the rich and poor. It is the apparent inequality of the classes.

Let's face it. Various individuals and families enjoy the benefits of material possessions, financial success, educational opportunities, and prestige. However, others suffer need, hunger, disease, and ignorance due to their economic situation. Poverty is a sad fact of this world, an enduring plague!

But what are the causes of poverty? What causes success? These important questions have produced new political theories, volumes of speculations, and even revolutionary movements throughout the world.

Many people believe wealth is limited. It has been unequally distributed. To balance the rich-poor gap, we must redistribute the world's wealth equally. Some political activists also believe evil is caused by an unjust external system. For them the external—society, government, etc.—causes moral problems. Man is evil because of his system.

Many of these ideas contain perfect logic. But it is possible that some of the premises are based on false ideas. Is wealth limited? Does the fact that one man is rich cause another to be poor? Does a first-world economy depend upon a system of exploitation and craftiness? Have the wicked rich collected an unfair portion of the world's wealth and left the poor lacking? Do the rich cause poverty?

Could it be that wealth is not limited? Maybe it is created. Would that not be good news for the poor? Is it possible that new wealth is unlimited in ideas, inventions, and honest work in service to others? Suppose a prosperous man is not evil. But how could that be?

Wealth Can Be Created!

You need *ideas, character*, and a *government* that protects your opportunities.

Ideas

Ideas are the primary source for the creation of wealth. Every person is created in the image of God and possesses a unique source of creativity, a well of unending ideas. Wealth is only as limited as one's ideas or as limitless as his creative genius.

Natural resources do not cause the creation of wealth. Oil was not considered a resource until someone invented the internal combustion engine. Today's greatly expanding computer industry has among some of its complex components the microchip. This chip is made of silicon, a mere element of sand! If natural resources were the cause of wealth, then Japan and other East Asian-rim nations would still be very poor. They are almost devoid of natural resources.

The human spirit is the primary source of the creation of wealth. People need not be passive as they meet the challenges of oppression and poverty. Prosperity wells up from the bottom: from ideas, inventiveness, and activities of millions of small business artists. Creating a small business is a true art!

Good business ideas must serve the real needs of others to be successful. The creation of wealth is not a mere selfish activity, but rather a unique opportunity to creatively serve others.

Character

Character is a moral quality. It is the sum of a person's thought life, actions, habits, and motives. This is a self-made pattern of thought and behavior. Your character affects the quality of your ideas and creativity. Pure thoughts and motives are necessary seeds in the fruitful garden of successful businesses. Men were designed by God to be good stewards of His creation. Man is to be a faithful trustee, transforming raw materials in order to be of a greater value and service to other human beings.

Men must use diligence, discipline and wise planning to produce wealth, not merely consume it. One must take risks, make sacrifices, and work hard. Evil men may be guilty of greed and withholding a just wage from their employees to amass more wealth, but it takes a man of virtue to earn and create wealth which serves society. Compassion for the poor is a virtuous character quality which seeks to alleviate poverty. A compassionate man will seek to establish ways to encourage economic development among the teeming ranks of the poor.

Government

The purpose of civil government is to protect and serve its citizens. A just government will not seize or usurp the people's means of creating wealth. The state ought to exist for man, not man for the state.

God has given people talents without regard to social status. He has given internal gifts to the poor that lie waiting to be developed. Society ought to arrange itself to provide opportunities for the poor to express their hidden talents. The government must be committed to ensure that the poor and needy have every opportunity and protection to pursue the productive enterprise of their abilities and ideas. The poor must not be thought of as seeking their slice of the "limited-wealth pie." Society will actually be enhanced by their success.

Government must discipline itself to serve and support moral and economic development. Creativity may be discouraged through excessive taxes. However, responsible taxation will provide for the proper function of the state's limited role in economic development. A just government is necessary to curtail the unjust gain of the wicked and their exploitation of the creativity of others. Crime must not prosper!

The state should respect the ownership rights of its individual citizens. Wise government will understand that, while it cannot legislate morality of the heart, it may inhibit immorality through proper laws and consequences. Governmental, moral, and economic institutions should not compete but rather join hands, working hard to create a just and caring society.

What Is the Cause of Poverty?

Unjust oppression of the poor is but one of many reasons for the existence of destructive poverty. Poverty is often the result of a person's own bad habits and character. It may be caused by wickedness, drunkenness, frivolity, immorality, impulsiveness, miserliness, and pure laziness. Some are innocent victims of poverty. There are women and children abandoned by irresponsible fathers. Greedy men sometimes commit horrid injustices against honest men. And yet it is a sad fact that too many are willful and responsible participants in their own poverty and destruction. Therefore, to reach out to help many of the poor is an act of mercy and grace. Others that have been sinned against must be justly defended. Government must encourage and reward both those who reach out in mercy and those who justly defend!

Liberating the Poor

So, if wealth is indeed created, it is not limited. This is good news for the poor, for as they turn to God for help, He promises to provide them their needs according to His limitless riches in glory. He will give them ideas and help them develop a character and a wise strategy of stewardship. Liberating the poor from the devastating moral bondage of sin, and protecting them from sins against them, is a major key in alleviating poverty. They need not take up arms to forcibly take their "piece of the pie." But they do need an opportunity to create the wealth to meet their needs.

Government must be fashioned by man to serve man. Man is of greater value than the state. The state's job is to protect from tyranny and provide freedom of opportunities for the poor to express their creative talents. They should be encouraged to participate in the liberation from their own poverty.

The rich should be encouraged by both moral and political institutions to give to the poor, helping to train, educate and provide opportunities to start small businesses. As the poor rise out of poverty, they should be encouraged to help others. Wealth is a means to an end, not an end in itself. The creation of wealth is the most powerful means available for the liberation of the poor from the tyranny and destruction of grinding poverty!

When creating wealth remains the means, the end will always be *liberty!*

© 1989

Note: Don is a missionary with YWAM, working in a developing country. We acknowledge that this is a complex issue, but our space limitations do not allow Don to deal with other correlating factors, such as the correct implementation of ideas and the availability of resources and training for success. —*Loren Cunningham*

Notes

Chapter 5: The King of Wall Street

1. Taken primarily from an interview in July 1988 with Betty Hall of Alta, California, one of only around twelve hundred descendants of the Shasta Indians.

2. Loren Cunningham, *Making Jesus Lord* (Seattle: YWAM Publishing, 1988), 103.

Chapter 6: How to Keep from Crashing

1. Actual names have been changed.

2. Wayne E. Warner, *Touched by the Fire: Eyewitness Accounts of the Early Twentieth Century Pentecostal Revival* (Plainfield, N.J.: Logos International, 1978), 25–27.

3. "Cause for Soul-searching," *The United Methodist Reporter* (Nov. 16, 1990).

Chapter 7: God's Practical Economics

1. *The Christian Century* (Dec. 14, 1988): 1140–1141.

2. Ibid.

3. *National Review* (Mar. 10, 1989): 44.

4. I am indebted to my friend Rod Gerhart for the delineation of these four categories, which I have adapted.

Chapter 8: Missions Support, the Jesus Way

1. See 1 Corinthians 9 and 2 Corinthians 8 and 9.

2. David B. Barrett and Todd M. Johnson, *Our Globe and How to Reach It* (Birmingham, Ala.: New Hope, 1990), 25.

Chapter 9: Living by Faith in the Nine-to-Five World

1. See "The Creation of Wealth and the Alleviation of Poverty" in the appendix.

Chapter 10: How to Give

1. Loren Cunningham, *Making Jesus Lord* (Seattle: YWAM Publishing, 1988).

Chapter 11: Invisible Means of Support

1. My first book was written on this subject: *Is That Really You, God?* (Seattle: YWAM Publishing, 1984).

Chapter 12: How to Ask for Money

1. Written by Adrian Plass, a regular columnist in *Christian Family* magazine. For a sample copy, write to 37 Elm Road, New Malden, Surrey KT3 3HB, England.

About the Author

Loren Cunningham is the founder of Youth With A Mission (YWAM), a missions organization with nearly twenty thousand full-time staff of more than 150 nationalities and from a wide variety of denominations. Loren has ministered in every sovereign nation and dependent country in the world as well as scores of territories and islands. Loren and his wife, Darlene, live in Kona, Hawaii. Together they serve in leadership capacities in YWAM and YWAM's University of the Nations. They have two adult children and three grandchildren. Loren is the author of four other books: *Is that Really You, God?*; *Making Jesus Lord*; *Why Not Women?* (with David Hamilton); and *The Book That Transforms Nations*.

Other Books by Loren Cunningham

THE BOOK THAT TRANSFORMS NATIONS
The Power of the Bible to Change Any Country
                                        by Loren Cunningham, $14.99
"God's love for all the nations of the earth is conveyed through Loren's intriguing factual accounts and real-life stories. In face of seemingly ever-increasing spiritual darkness worldwide, this book provides hope and a reminder of the power of the Bible."
                —Joyce Meyer, best-selling author and Bible teacher
"The Book That Transforms Nations is both a reminder of what God has done in the past as well as practical in what every believer can do. Loren Cunningham will ignite your imagination and renew hope in you for the world."
                —Rick Warren, author, *The Purpose Driven Life*
(ISBN 978-1-57658-183-4)

WHY NOT WOMEN?
A Fresh Look at Scripture on Women in Missions,
Ministry, and Leadership
                by Loren Cunningham and David Hamilton, $15.99
Why Not Women? brings light, not just more heat, to the church's crucial debate with a detailed study of women in Scripture, historical and current global perspectives, an examination of the fruit of women in public ministry, and a powerful evaluation of what's at stake for women, men, the body of Christ, God's kingdom, and the unreached. (ISBN 978-1-57658-183-4)

IS THAT REALLY YOU, GOD?
Hearing the Voice of God
                                        by Loren Cunningham, $9.99
This practical guide to hearing God's voice shows how an ordinary man who was committed to hearing God and obeying Him became the founder of the largest interdenominational missions organization in the world. (ISBN 978-1-57658-244-2)

MAKING JESUS LORD
The Dynamic Power of Laying Down Your Rights

by Loren Cunningham, $9.99

We live in a world in which the protection and exaltation of individual rights has become an obsession. As Christians we believe that personal rights do hold great value. As a result, we can perform no greater act of faith and worship than to consciously lay down these rights at the feet of the One who has gone before us, Jesus Himself! Loren Cunningham details proven steps to a transformed life of freedom, joy, and intimate fellowship with God. Includes study guide. (ISBN 978-1-57658-012-7)

Other Books from YWAM Publishing

HIS KINGDOM COME
An Integrated Approach to Discipling the Nations and Fulfilling the Great Commission
> by Jim Stier, Richlyn Poor, Lisa Orvis, eds., $24.99

With biblical, historical, and stategic insights gleaned from some thirty contributing authors, this book will open your eyes to what God has been doing in Christian missions worldwide regarding Christ's mandate to "make disciples of all nations" (Matt. 28:19).

"This volume will reveal the vision, passion, and innovation that is enabling God to use YWAM to alleviate suffering, impact communities, and extend the kingdom of God all over the world. The reader will be impressed that the task of discipling the nations is not for an elite few who go as professional missionaries but is the responsibility of every church and every believer."
—Jerry Rankin, President, International Mission Board, SBC
(ISBN 978-1-57658-435-4)

BUSINESS AS MISSION
The Power of Business in the Kingdom of God
> by Michael R. Baer, $12.99

Is it possible for concerned Christian businesspeople to successfully bring kingdom purposes into their professional lives? With fresh insight, Michael Baer challenges the separation between sacred and secular, introducing readers to useful concepts that can transform the workplace and world for Christ.
(ISBN 978-1-57658-388-3)

MANIFESTO
Revolutionary Christianity for a Postmodern World
> by Olu Robbin-Coker, $14.99

Born and raised in Sierra Leone and now living in Scotland, Olu Robbin-Coker offers a personal, biblical, even revolutionary evaluation of Christian belief in a postmodern world. Explore in unconventional ways what it means to know God, know yourself, be part of the church, and live in the world while embracing God's coming kingdom. (ISBN 978-1-57658-471-2)

YOU SEE BONES, I SEE AN ARMY
Changing the Way We Do Church
by Floyd McClung, $14.99

Why are frustrated church members leaving their congregations? What can be done about it? In this thought-provoking, timely book, Floyd McClung presents principles of leadership, church, and mission sure to challenge believers, redefine the church, and bring about real change. (ISBN 978-1-57658-438-5)

RELATIONSHIPS
The Key to Love, Sex, and Everything Else
by Dean Sherman, $12.99

With clarity and a sharp wit, Dean Sherman illuminates the confusing and mysterious world of love, sex, and relationships in this accessible, hard-hitting examination of romantic love and sexuality in the Christian's life. Includes study guide.
(ISBN 978-1-57658-275-6)

BECOMING A WORLD CHANGING FAMILY
Fun & Innovative Ways to Spread the Good News
Donna S. Thomas, $11.99

With a wealth of ideas that are fun and practical, this book shows how to help children appreciate people of all cultures and see the world as Jesus does. Families will be challenged to become world changers, bringing the transforming message of Christ to those around them. (ISBN 978-1-57658-452-1)

SPIRITUAL WARFARE FOR EVERY CHRISTIAN
How to Live in Victory and Retake the Land
by Dean Sherman, $12.99

God has called Christians to overcome the world and drive back the forces of evil and darkness at work within it. Spiritual warfare isn't just casting out demons; it's Spirit-controlled thinking and attitudes. Dean delivers a no-nonsense, both-feet-planted-on-the-ground approach to the unseen world. Includes study guide. (ISBN 978-0-927545-05-1)

DISCIPLING NATIONS
The Power of Truth to Transform Cultures
by Darrow L. Miller, $15.99
The power of the Gospel to transform individual lives has been clearly evident throughout New Testament history. But what of the darkness and poverty that enslave entire cultures? In *Discipling Nations*, Darrow Miller builds a powerful and convincing thesis that God's truth not only breaks the spiritual bonds of sin and death but can free whole societies from deception and poverty. Excellent study of worldviews. Includes study guide. (ISBN 978-1-57658-248-0)

COURAGEOUS LEADERS
Transforming Their World
by James Halcomb, David Hamilton, and Howard Malmstadt, $15.99
Our world needs courageous leaders who will recognize the need for God-motivated action and follow through with a God-led plan. Whether your vision for change is local or global, simple or complex, for home, business, or ministry, *Courageous Leaders* will help you remain on a true course and reach the goal set before you. (ISBN 978-1-57658-171-1)

THE LEADERSHIP PARADOX
A Challenge to Servant Leadership in a Power Hungry World
by Denny Gunderson, $11.99
What is the key to effective leadership? The ability to organize and take charge? The ability to preach and teach? Entrepreneurial skill? A charismatic personality? According to Jesus, none of the above. This refreshingly candid book draws us to the Master's side. Through the eyes of people who experienced Jesus firsthand, we discover insights that will challenge us to rethink our leadership stereotypes. Includes study guide. (ISBN 978-1-57658-379-1)

INTENSIVE DISCIPLESHIP COURSE
The Perfect Course for Students Who Are Serious about Following God

by Vinnie Carafano, $14.99 each

Developed from years of student ministry experience, the Intensive Discipleship Course is designed specifically for high school and college students who are hungry to know God more, dive deep into His Word, and discover His plan for their lives. Each volume in the series is a twelve-week, life-changing exercise of commitment and learning. *(More volumes coming soon.)*

Developing Godly Character

Students will establish a firm foundation for effectively studying the Bible, developing a strong prayer life, serving in humility, overcoming sin, and growing spiritually. (ISBN 978-1-57658-410-1)

Being Useful to God Now

Students will learn to be active, effective disciples of Christ—*right now*—by living out God's love and compassion, studying evangelism techniques, counseling peers through life-controlling problems, and hearing God's call on their lives.
(ISBN 978-1-57658-470-5)

INTERNATIONAL ADVENTURES
True Stories of Spiritual Victory and Personal Triumph

by various authors, $12.99 each

On every continent, in every nation, God is at work in and through the lives of believers. From the streets of Amsterdam to remote Pacific islands to the jungles of Ecuador and beyond, each international adventure that emerges is a dramatic episode that could be directed only by the hand of God.

Against All Odds • 978-0-927545-44-0
A Cry from the Streets • 978-1-57658-263-3
Dayuma: Life Under Waorani Spears • 978-0-927545-91-4
Imprisoned in Iran • 978-1-57658-180-3
Living on the Devil's Doorstep • 978-0-927545-45-7
Lords of the Earth • 978-1-57658-290-9
The Man with the Bird on His Head • 978-1-57658-005-9

Peace Child • 978-1-57658-289-3
Taking the High Places • 978-1-57658-412-5
Tomorrow You Die • 978-0-927545-92-1
Torches of Joy • 978-0-927545-43-3
Totally Surrounded • 978-1-57658-165-0
Walking Miracle • 978-1-57658-455-2

CHRISTIAN HEROES: THEN & NOW
Great missionary biographies for younger readers as well as adults!

by Janet and Geoff Benge, $8.99 each

This popular series chronicles the exciting, challenging, and deeply touching true stories of ordinary men and women whose trust in God accomplished extraordinary exploits for His kingdom and glory. Real people—incredible, inspiring true stories for ages 10 and up.

Brother Andrew • 978-1-57658-355-5
Gladys Aylward • 978-1-57658-019-6
Rowland Bingham • 978-1-57658-282-4
Corrie ten Boom • 978-1-57658-136-0
William Booth • 978-1-57658-258-9
David Bussau • 978-1-57658-415-6
William Carey • 978-1-57658-147-6
Amy Carmichael • 978-1-57658-018-9
Loren Cunningham • 978-1-57658-199-5
Jim Elliot • 978-1-57658-146-9
Jonathan Goforth • 978-1-57658-174-2
Betty Greene • 978-1-57658-152-0
Wilfred Grenfell • 978-1-57658-292-3
Clarence Jones • 978-1-57658-343-2
Adoniram Judson • 978-1-57658-161-2
C. S. Lewis • 978-1-57658-385-2
Eric Liddell • 987-1-57658-137-7
David Livingstone • 978-1-57658-153-7
Lottie Moon • 978-1-57658-188-9
George Müller • 978-1-57658-145-2
Nate Saint • 978-1-57658-017-2

Rachel Saint • 978-1-57658-337-1
Ida Scudder • 978-1-57658-285-5
Sundar Singh • 978-1-57658-318-0
Mary Slessor • 978-1-57658-148-3
C. T. Studd • 978-1-57658-288-6
Hudson Taylor • 978-1-57658-016-5
Cameron Townsend • 978-1-57658-164-3
Lillian Trasher • 978-1-57658-305-0
John Wesley • 978-1-57658-382-1
John Williams • 978-1-57658-256-5
Florence Young • 978-1-57658-313-5
Count Zinzendorf • 978-1-57658-262-6

**Call 1-800-922-2143 for a full catalog,
or visit www.ywampublishing.com.**